FROM BEATINGS TO BLESSINGS

Printed and bound by Lightning Source, Milton Keynes, UK

Published by Crossbridge Books
Berrow Green, Martley
WR6 6PL
Tel: +44 (0)1886 821128

© Crossbridge Books 2010

First published 2010
Previously published as The Reluctant Bride

ISBN 978 0 9561787 4 9

British Library Cataloguing in Publication Data.
A catalogue record for this book is available from
the British Library.

Also published by **CROSSBRIDGE BOOKS**:

The God of Miracles Trevor and Anne Dearing
Called to Be a Wife Anne Dearing
Stepping-Stone Miracles Des Morton
Mother Twin Eileen Mohr
Schizophrenia Defeated James Stacey

FROM BEATINGS
TO BLESSINGS

Kamala Sabaratnam
with
Patricia Turnage

CROSSBRIDGE
BOOKS

Foreword

A few ladies from Socketts Heath Baptist Church in Grays meet for Bible study each Wednesday morning. After coffee and biscuits and a light-hearted chat, we begin serious Bible study. We have much to share and have grown together in knowledge and strength in our spiritual walk. There is always plenty of laughter and fun in our gatherings, largely caught from the smiling brightness of our leader, Kamala. She presides in her armchair in the corner of the fellowship room, rotund and motherly, her dark eyes wide and shining. There's no trace of a line in her silky brown countenance. Her black hair and calm radiance belie her 62 years and the physical suffering she has to continually endure.

"I had been working nights for some time and was very tired," she says, as she begins to relate one of her experiences in her soft eastern lilt. "An old lady had been calling out for the bedpan all night. Angela, the auxiliary nurse, would walk the whole length of the ward to take it to her, and each time the old lady would tell her that she didn't need it.

"We sat quietly chatting in the early morning, exhausted after a busy night. Once more the dreaded cry came:

" 'Nurse, please bring me a bedpan.'

"I was worn out and at the end of my tether. Angela looked amazed as she watched me take a pillow from a pile in the corner. I laid it on the floor and jumped up and down on it until it was as flat as a pancake! Then I kicked it all down the ward with all my might. When I reached the old lady's bed, I drew a deep breath, smoothed out my apron and was able to ask her very sweetly:

" 'Yes, my darling, what is it you wanted?'

"Angela had watched everything and fell about laughing. She couldn't get up off the floor, her sides ached so much!"

We joined Kamala in her laughter and she clapped her hand over her mouth to stifle her shrieks.

Kamala's strong faith and sense of humour have upheld her through many bitter experiences. I have been so impressed by her glowing faith and courage in the face of adversity and strong resolve to serve the Lord, that I felt prompted to ask her if I might help her to write her story.

"The Lord must be in this," she replied, "for I have been praying that He would help me to record my experiences."

So it is with extreme confidence and faith in His leading that I present to you Kamala's amazing story. I hope it will be as great a blessing to you as it has been to me and many others.

Pat Turnage.

v

Acknowledgements

We wish to thank Viv and Tim Lee
and Ruth Elmer for all their help and
encouragement with the manuscript.

K.S. and P.T.

Biblical quotations
are taken from
The Holy Bible, New King James Version
Copyright 1982 by Thomas Nelson, Inc.

Contents

Introduction

GOD IS SO REAL and part of my life. Without God's loving kindness my existence would be of no worth. My heart is overwhelmed with a desire to testify to God's goodness to me. Many times have I cried out to Him in my need to share my testimony with others. I wanted to put my experiences in writing to help others who may be having the same kind of problems.

"Blessed be the God and Father of our Lord Jesus Christ, the Father of mercies and God of all comfort, who comforts us in all our tribulation, that we may be able to comfort those who are in any trouble, with the comfort with which we ourselves are comforted by God". (2 Corinthians 1: 2-4)

One Wednesday morning when we had finished our Ladies' Bible Study session, Pat, my friend and dear sister in the Lord, approached me with some blank audio cassette tapes in her hand. She quietly asked me if I could record my experiences onto the tapes so that she could write about them. I was so amazed, because even that morning I had cried out to God and beseeched Him to do something with my testimonies or else my heart would burst! Yet again, God had answered my prayer.

As a result of my friend's love and dedication of her time and efforts this book is born. I want to thank Pat, and her husband Roy who always picked me up by car and provided lunch, and then took me home, to enable us to work on the story. I am always grateful to them.

I would especially like to dedicate this book to my parents for all their love and support. My father is with the Lord, and since completing this book, my mother went to join him at the age of 97, but not before fulfilling her desire to read my story.

And so I commend to you this account of my experiences in the hope that those who read it will find God and live in His love and comfort as I have done for so many years.

Kamala Sabaratnam

CHAPTER 1

Broken dreams

It was the summer of 1958. I was returning home from college with my friends in a hired car, bumping along the dusty road in the stifling tropical heat, oblivious to what awaited me. I knew nothing then of the sorrow and suffering I was destined to endure and that this fateful journey would prove to be the beginning of a longer, spiritual journey of pain and hardship.

Our Hindu doctrine maintains that our suffering in this life is fate and the result of sins committed in our previous life. In the days that lay ahead, I was to wonder about my own fate and what I must have done to deserve such suffering and pain.

As we rode along on the thirty-minute journey home, my mind was full of concerns that normally preoccupy a sixteen-year-old. I was enjoying my studies and hoped to go on to higher education. The car jogged along a tarmac road and onto the chalky roads of the small village of Sandirupay. We passed the primary school, which held so many memories, the familiar Co-operative store, the grocers and the bicycle shop.

I watched the people as they passed one of the three temples in the village. They would each pause, shake off their shoes and bow their heads with hands devoutly clasped in pious reverence to the holy shrines. Opposite one of the temples, boys were playing football in a large playground, religious disciplines far from their minds.

The chalky roads gradually gave way to a winding, sandy lane, hemmed each side by fences made from large, intertwined palmyra leaves and overhung by jasmine, coconut palms and margosa trees. The stifling air was pungent with their scents, mingling with the strong aroma of cooking spices wafting from the large, square houses nestling either side of the fence.

As usual, at about 4 o'clock each weekday, the car finally lurched to a standstill outside the large iron gates of our house. I said goodbye to my friends and pushed open the gates. I would always visit Vasugi, my friend next door before carrying out my usual household chores. Then I would wash and go to the main reception room to pray to the pictures of the gods which hung on the whitewashed walls. It was a custom I never questioned, but accepted as part of family life, as well as the special days of prayer and periodic visits to the temple. After prayer, I would do my homework before joining the family for the evening meal at 7 p.m.

Our house was large, consisting of one story laid out in a square, with rooms opening out onto an inner verandah surrounding an open courtyard in the centre, with another verandah running along the front of the house. It was set in extensive grounds, ablaze with reds and golds of hibiscus and jasmine and the pinks and mauves of the bright, luxuriant bougainvillea, which cascaded over its sun-baked walls.

As I entered the gates on that fateful afternoon, I could see there were visitors on the front verandah and immediately assumed that friends of my father were gathering. He had a weakness for alcohol and enjoyed inviting people to our house for eating and drinking and merriment. Unbeknown to his children, he was spending all our mother's wealth. It was the custom that children, particularly girls, should not speak to visitors unless they knew them very well.

To avoid meeting them, I squeezed through a screen fence to the left of the gate and went around to the back of the house. I entered through the back door to find my brother, Mahendran, eagerly awaiting my arrival.

"Some people have come to see you to discuss a proposal of marriage!" he cried, his face alight and eager to pass on the news.

I was shocked and bewildered, at a complete loss to know whether or not he was teasing me.

"No, you mustn't tease me like that, Mahendran."

3

"I'm not teasing you. It's true!" he insisted.

"Yes, it is true, Kamala."

I turned to see the tall, serene figure of my mother standing in the doorway.

"But, Mother, I must continue my education and achieve something in my life. I have no intention of marrying yet!" I cried.

"Don't worry, I will never allow you to marry until you have finished college," she assured me.

My father had other ideas, and my mother had no power to prevent him promising me in marriage to Kumar, whom I had never even met, and who, at 32, was twice my age.

My elder sister, Theivanayaki, had married at the age of 18, but I did not want to enter into marriage at such a young age. My parents were high caste Hindus and followed the age-old custom of arranged marriages.

They believed it would keep their children from misbehaving and choosing wrong partners. Even though most marriages proved successful, I did not want to conform or fit into such traditions, where astrological charts were kept of each child and referred to when choosing a partner. Educational standards, wealth, caste, age and character were taken into consideration when arranging such a match.

The practice was to register the marriage one year before the actual wedding. My elder brother, Kandasamy, would also have to register, as it was an inter-marriage. It was arranged for him to marry

4

Kumar's sister.

My brother was equally opposed to the idea, as he was only 26 and had just started working in Colombo. Our continuous protests were to no avail and we both reluctantly bowed to our father's wishes. Although he was a loving father, he was eager to offload his financial responsibilities.

The day of registration came and both families gathered at our home, with the Registrar in attendance. As I approached the table to sign the register I saw Kumar for the first time. He looked much older than I had imagined. A slight, quirky smile momentarily enlivened his dark face, but failed to reach his eyes as he greeted me politely.

My voice was just above a whisper as I hesitantly returned his greeting. From that moment I had a deep sense of foreboding. Afterwards, I told my parents that I had had a premonition that my promised husband would be cruel and that they would later regret pushing me into such a pit of despair. I insisted that I would be losing my virginity to someone I knew I could never love. Still my protests fell upon deaf ears.

During the period of registration, Kumar visited me frequently. I was too frightened to meet him alone as I sensed his aggressiveness and asked Mahendran to sit in on the meetings. The custom of registration is as binding as marriage, and I was so terrified that I asked my parents if I could be divorced.

5

Their response was to bring the marriage forward a few months, and to my dismay, they arranged for the wedding to take place later that year on 1st December 1958. My brother would be marrying Kumar's sister five months later. Instead of joy I felt deep sadness and fear. Instead of taking my final exams at college, I was to be imprisoned in a marriage with someone whom I knew I could never love.

CHAPTER 2

Serendipity

Legend tells us that India was once a beautiful woman's face. She shed a tear of joy which froze in mid-air as it fell into the Indian Ocean. That tear became the beautiful island of Sri Lanka, originally named Serendib. Horace Walpole, an 18th-Century English writer, had Sri Lanka in mind when he coined the word "serendipity" — the faculty of making happy and unexpected discoveries.

It is indeed a bright, vibrant country packed with unexpected delights, tumbling waterfalls and green mountain slopes. It is a land of dramatic, tropical beauty, rich in culture and history, yet smaller than Ireland. The lush greens of the mountains and surrounding tea plantations rise high above a carpet of grass, brush and forest. I lived in the Northern Province in the village of Sandirupay, with my father and mother and grandmother, three brothers and elder sister.

I had enjoyed a serendipity of my own during

my happy and secure childhood years. My father was always loving and caring, not only towards his family but to anybody who came through the door. He was kind and generous, even to the lower castes and would always feed the hungry. They were not allowed to come inside the houses of those of higher caste, nor were they permitted to go into the temples. Nowadays, however, the barriers have been broken down and people mix more freely with those of lower caste.

My father would exercise discipline and smack the boys, but never laid a hand on me nor my elder sister, Theivanayaki. He was greatly loved by friends, neighbours and relatives alike and very well known in the area as a Shraff in the Land Registry Office. This post would be equivalent to an officer in the Civil Service in England. Later, when he retired at the age of 55, he took the job of Registrar of births, deaths and marriages. His only weakness was for parties and drinking. He did not take life as seriously as my mother.

As far back as I can remember, my mother was very hard-working and lived by strict principles. She dedicated her life to her family and always desired the best education for us. My father did not want me to study beyond primary school and progress to secondary school in the normal way, as he thought further education was unnecessary for a girl after the age of thirteen. He maintained this would incur unnecessary expense, paying for college fees, books, clothes and the cost of a hired car to and from college.

He told the principal of the primary school that he was not to transfer my leaving certificate to the college which I wished to attend. My mother was furious. Although she did not want me to go to the designated secondary school, she was determined that I should attend a special ladies college to further my education. She went along to see the head of the primary school. When he refused to give her the certificate, she faced him angrily across his desk.

"You cannot hold on to Kamala's certificate. If you do not hand it over, I will go straight to the law. You have no right to refuse me."

Confronted by this tall, angular lady with large, flashing eyes, quivering with firm resolve, the Principal gave in gracefully and immediately relinquished my certificate. And so, contrary to my father's wishes, my mother ensured that I went to the college of her choice.

She also ensured that we had a happy and disciplined home life. My three brothers and I (my sister had married and left home when I was six years old) all had our separate chores to perform before we left for school each morning.

Firstly, we would have a shower just outside the house within the compound. Not for us the showers like we use in the West, where at the turn of a tap we stand beneath its invigorating spray. We had to lower a bucket into the well and draw it up full of water.

Then we would dip a basin into the bucket and throw the water over ourselves.

In the cold season, in February and March, when the temperature was around 60°F (15°C), we would heat the water in a copper cauldron over a fire which we built outside.

We would also draw water from the well to use for washing-up and cooking etc. Cows were regarded as holy, and we possessed one cow and two goats. It was the responsibility of Mahendran to feed them with leaves from the trees which my youngest brother, Pathmanathan would collect. My job was to sweep the whole house.

We had to repeat the chores when we returned home from school in the late afternoon. The inner courtyard, which was covered by a roof of netting to keep out the birds, and the grounds were cleaned by local helpers from the lower caste people.

Our grandmother always went to collect the harvest from the fields we owned. The fields were looked after by leaseholders, and at harvest time Grandmother would oversee the collection of the rice, sesame seed and hay which was transported by bullocarts and stored in a room in the house. She would sit strong and stately beneath her colourful umbrella astride the bags of rice and seed, majestically swaying from side to side as the bullocart slowly bore her home.

We worked hard and played hard, and especially looked forward to the school holidays when my aunt's children came to visit. We would play games in the large grounds of the house and in the sandy lane outside. During the monsoon, the same sandy lane became a flowing river in which we splashed delightedly. We showered beneath drainpipes at each corner of the roof of the inner courtyard.

Many of our games are also enjoyed by the children in England: hopscotch, five stones, football, cricket and hide and seek. I especially enjoyed playing mummies and daddies, building houses out of sticks from the trees, and using leaves for the roof. We built a fire outside and cooked rice in small clay pots. I was quite a tomboy and played a lot with my brothers and the boys of the neighbourhood, climbing the mango and jackfruit trees, using our catapults to pelt the birds and squirrels.

We also looked forward to our annual family holiday at the seaside. We lived about six miles from the northern coast and each year my mother would book a room in a large lodge overlooking the sea. It cost us nothing as the house, which was built like a hostel, had been donated by a rich Shraff for the use of anyone who wanted to visit the seaside. He was a most generous benefactor. There was a supply of buttermilk at the gate of the building for passers-by to drink. This practice was still carried out after his death, using funds he left for the charity.

We would get up at about 4 a.m. each morning when the beach was shrouded in heavy morning mist, and run barefoot through the white sand before plunging into the cool, invigorating waves. In this way we were able to teach ourselves to swim. At about 8 a.m. we ran back to the house for Mum's special breakfast of idiappam or stringhoppers. These were made with rice flour made into dough and pushed through tiny holes in a mould, emerging as strings onto circular, bamboo trays. The long strands were then steamed and served with coconut and chilli chutney known as "sambol", and with "sothi", a coconut sauce.

It was all homemade and my mother had to rise early to prepare and serve it all steaming hot. Afterwards we would play in the grounds until lunch. With temperatures of 90-100°F (32-38°C) it was a relief to feel the cool breeze from the sea. After lunch we had a siesta from 2-4 p.m., then back to the beach with snacks until 9 p.m. It was idyllic.

I would spend the remainder of the holiday with my sister, Theivanayaki. She was the fair, good-looking one of the family. I was always known as the dark one! I always looked forward to visiting her and spent much time playing with her three children. I was seven years old when Bhavani, her eldest girl was born, then came Satha, a little boy, followed by the youngest daughter, Nalayini.

Theivanayaki was always so sweet and kind. I will always remember how she spent such a lot of her time making me beautiful dresses. She was always very hard working and careful with money, making her own clothes, recycling everything and wasting nothing. When she lived at home, she would milk the cow (something I could never do) and sell the milk as well as fruit from the garden. She also kept hens which she would sell.

I have many memories of my mother working hard at home in the kitchen. After my father had retired, he would help her when he could. Each morning he would bring in the firewood and leave it next to the cooker. There were two cookers side by side on a stone platform on one side of the kitchen heated by a fire beneath. An array of clay cooking pots were perched on top. My father would get up at about 4.30 a.m., light the kerosene lamp and take it into the kitchen, sweep the floor and clean out the ashes from the cookers. After this, he would wash and shine the brass tumblers, milk the cow, boil the milk and put on the kettle to make the coffee.

In the evening he would sit warming himself by the kitchen fire while he fed it with more wood from the pile beside the cooker. I remember this always agitated my mother as he was in her way when she set about cooking the evening meal. As well as firewood he would put coconut husks and shells and also dried palmyra seeds and leaves onto the fire.

One day, my mother put some wet palmyra seeds in the pile. Not realising the seeds were wet, my father threw a handful onto the fire. My mother watched with great delight as her plan began to work. The fire was transformed into a cascading mass of exploding seeds, sending my father somersaulting backwards out of the kitchen door. He landed in a confused heap outside, vowing never to go near the fire again!

Tobacco is grown in Sri Lanka and sold in the market. My father made cheroots which he smoked after meals and when out walking. His was a familiar figure strolling along the dusty paths of the village clad in a white shirt and verti (a long length of cotton draped to his ankles), deep in thought and puffing at a cheroot. Even my mother was not averse to the weed and would quietly puff away in the early morning and just before bedtime when the house was quiet.

One day, a man called at the house and asked to see my father, the Registrar. He offered my father money to falsify a birth certificate. My father flatly refused, but the man would not take no for an answer and kept coming back to plead for his request to be granted. Each time, much to our amusement, my father would hide and send us to the gate to make excuses.

But the day came when the man came through the gate unannounced. It was the day when Mahendran chose to be very naughty and my father was chasing him round and round the connecting verandahs at the back, angrily wielding a stick. Suddenly Mahendran shot through the hallway to the front verandah with his father hot on his heels just as our visitor was proceeding along the front path towards the house. At that moment Mahendran fled out of sight, and all the man could see was my angry father menacingly waving the stick. Suddenly my father caught sight of the unwelcome visitor, who immediately turned tail and ran straight out of the gate. Outside he bumped into a lady passing by.

"Why are you running?" she asked.

"Mr Sabaratnam is chasing me with a stick!" he cried as he fled down the lane in a cloud of dust.

My father threw down the stick and roared with laughter and Mahendran and the whole family joined in the mirth.

I was brought up in the Hindu tradition, accepting it as part of our family life, but I never thought very deeply about the meaning of it all. At New Year and Harvest celebrations we laid out a square pattern with flour in the courtyard and built a small wood fire in the centre on which we cooked rice to offer to the sun. We walked in procession around the square three times then bowed down to worship the sun. As children, we never took this too seriously, but enjoyed these special days which would culminate in an exciting display of fireworks.

Hinduism was taught at school as well as at home and the family would regularly attend the Hindu temple. I was familiar with all the rituals. When I entered the temple I would dip my finger into the sandalwood cream provided and put it on my forehead. This was called pottu. On top of that I would put a dot of red kumkum powder which is known as the third eye of Siva.

There were several gods to be worshipped in the temple, as I remember. Siva has three eyes and sits on a cow. His wife is called Parwarthy, his son is Ganesha who has the face of an elephant. Another son, Murugan, sits on a peacock. He has six heads with twelve arms, carved in black polished stone. He has two wives. On special occasions, the priest would wash the idols with milk before dressing them in silk. People would take rice, beetlenut, cubes of camphor, bananas and banana leaves, fresh cow's milk, flowers and money to the temple to offer to a god as fulfilment of a vow made in times of illness or trouble.

Usually, Gurus were more devout and set apart. They went on pilgrimages to India, fasted and chanted and prayed and lived in an ashram, which was like a monastery. The ordinary people visited the Gurus, addressing them as Swami, which is similar to the word used for 'god'. They listened to the Gurus' teaching, brought offerings and even invited them into their homes to bring blessings on the family. Gurus were much respected and it made us feel good to attend to their needs. Some took it to extremes and fell at their feet in worship, and in return the Gurus would bless them.

There were many books at home and in school containing the doctrines of the Gurus going back hundreds of years. Yet the Hindu religion is as multi-faceted as the jewel which is the island of Sri Lanka itself. There is no creed and the Hindu can believe what he wants and still be true to his faith. Although I read books and learned the doctrines at school, they proved to be more philosophical than practical and had no connection with my daily life. The rituals merely had the effect of making me feel momentarily pious. I was intent on studying and getting the best out of life. Now, everything seemed to be crashing down around my ears!

CHAPTER 3

Lamb to the slaughter

The wedding day arrived and we were getting ready to go to the Hindu temple, when a telegram came from my father's brother telling us that his son had drowned. According to Hindu custom, my parents would be unable to give me away as there had been a death in the family. Instead of providing me with a possible way of escape, the situation was swiftly resolved. My mother's sister and her husband volunteered to step in and give me away. To me, it all seemed like a bad omen and added to my distress.

All the food and snacks for the wedding celebrations were prepared a few days before. For me, the wedding began in the morning with a ritual bathing ceremony. My aunts and uncles blessed me by sprinkling milk and a special sacred grass on my head before bathing. Afterwards, my head was adorned with flowers and garlands and I put on a red silk sari, gold earrings, necklace and chain and

bangles. After this I had to stand in front of a pot of water on top of which sat a coconut on a bed of mango leaves. The pot itself stood on the table on top of a banana leaf with an oil lamp either side, each with five burning wicks. Two ladies then brought a tray on which were placed three pieces of banana, with wicks soaked in oil embedded in the centre of each. Beside these was placed a pot of beautifully fragrant sandalwood paste and one of red kumkum powder.

The ladies lit the wicks on the banana pieces and raised the tray up and down three times in front of me before extinguishing the flames. After this, one of the ladies dipped her finger into the sandalwood paste and placed a dot on my forehead. The other dipped her finger in the kumkum powder and pressed a dot on top of the sandalwood. This all took place before breakfast which was served on banana leaves. The banana leaf was used rather like a paper plate would be in Britain at parties and special occasions.

I had no appetite for breakfast and had to endure all the ceremonial Hindu customs with no thrill of anticipation, only deep foreboding. The time came to travel to the Hindu temple in a car, my face covered with a lace veil. The Hindu temple was lavishly decorated with flowers. I tried to smile sweetly as I joined Kumar and we sat before the Brahmin priest on a seat highly embellished with glittering ornaments.

19

The wedding ceremony was long and arduous and I could feel no joy or excitement. I seemed to be in a state of limbo and can remember little about the detail of the ceremony. I can recall the priest offering pujas to the gods by tossing flower petals from a bowl, chanting as he did so. In this way he invoked the blessing of the gods upon us and our marriage.

Then the fateful moment came when Kumar had to place the wedlock around my neck. It symbolised wedlock as the wedding ring does in this country, and was made of 9-11 sovereign coins of 22 carat gold. It was strung with Thali, the image of the god Ganesh shaped in gold dangling from the chain like charms on a bracelet. It had been blessed by the priest and visitors. Kumar had bought the chain as well as my sari and cosmetics as a gift, but I felt no thrill of happiness or shred of appreciation. As he tied the knot of the wedlock, I felt as though there was no way of escape. I was trapped and my fate was finally sealed.

The ceremony continued as I exchanged my flower garland with that of the bridegroom's and we both left the temple holding hands, followed by all the relatives. As we came out into the sunshine, I saw my father in his dazzling white verti which was folded around his waist in a special way, with a matching shirt and shawl emblazoned with borders of gold. My mother stood smiling, tall and serene in a striking red sari with gold motifs and borders, her hands folded in prayer. I felt an urge to run and hug them, for I desperately needed their comfort. Instead, I stood alone in my desolation as if I had been finally severed from them and the rest of the family.

We climbed into the car and made our way back to the house. On the way, we had to stop at a neighbour's house as was the custom. They had placed a table outside on which they had spread a tablecloth and placed a pot of water bearing a coconut standing on a banana leaf, in exactly the same way as in the morning ceremony before breakfast. They sprinkled scented water upon our heads in blessing before we went on to a second house where the ceremony was repeated. After this we continued on our way to my home where the wedding reception was held and where we would spend our first night.

Later, when we had said goodbye to the last lingering guest, the time which I had dreaded most had to be faced. I diffidently made my way to the bedroom with much fear and trepidation. Once in bed, I placed the blanket over my head and lay trembling. To my relief, after a gentle cuddle and a kiss, Kumar did not bother me and gradually went off to sleep.

As soon as I thought it was safe, I crawled out of bed and crept to my mother's bedroom. I quietly slipped into bed beside the sleeping form of my unsuspecting mother. I lay still, my heart pounding, not wanting to wake her. I held my breath as she turned and pressed against me. She immediately awoke and cried, "Who is that?"

"It's me," I squeaked.

"What are you doing here?" she screeched.

"Please, Mother, I am frightened."

"You must go straight back to your husband right now!" she ordered, yet her eyes were soft and twinkling and I stayed until early morning.

I sat at breakfast fearfully awaiting Kumar's arrival. He entered the room and I searched his face for some sign of displeasure. He sat pan faced, greeting us politely. Suddenly his face broadened into a big grin and with great relief I joined in the laughter. Thankfully, he was sympathetic. He had guessed what had happened and thought the whole thing hilariously funny.

We spent the remainder of the week at my husband's home a little way away. Having lost his parents and being the eldest son, he had had the responsibility of bringing up his brother and sisters and I noticed how bossy he was towards them. His brother, Ganeshan, worked as an Income Tax Assessor in Colombo and his two sisters, other than the one Kandasamy was to marry, were studying at boarding school.

We then travelled to Vavuniya, which was about 100 miles south of Jaffna, to our new flat in the country near the local health centre where my husband worked as an anti-malaria overseer. I cried so much. It was like separating a lamb from its mother. Now I had to learn to cook and do all the housework. I did not know the facts of life and three months later, when Kumar took me to visit my sister, I confided in her.

"I have not had a period for three months. Do you know what could be wrong?"

Theivanayaki looked at me quizzically, her eyes unable to disguise her suppressed amusement. "But Kamala, don't you know? You must be pregnant!"

Her words struck like a thunderbolt and I was completely stunned.

"However could this be?" I gasped in my innocence.

I was shocked at the realisation that a baby was living inside me. I found it so difficult to comprehend.

After I had been married five months, my mother and father came to Vavuniya to visit me. I was just leaving to go to a sewing class when I saw the car stop outside. I was so overjoyed to see Mum and Dad step out of the car that I threw down my sewing kit and ran to meet them. The car was laden with fruit and foodstuffs which they had brought, as was the custom during a daughter's pregnancy. When Kumar returned from work he too seemed pleased to see them. The joy I felt that day will never be erased from my heart.

That night, after my parents had returned home and we went to bed, Kumar became very uneasy and kept questioning me.

"I didn't know they were coming. Why did they

23

come?"

I could not understand his attitude, for up until then he had been really good to them. Admittedly, when we had visitors of any kind he would be very nice to their face, but after they had left he would be constantly criticising them.

The next morning at 6 a.m. he pulled me out of bed and started to kick me. He punched each side of my neck and kicked me in the stomach. I rolled about on the floor in pain, my heart beating fast. I was so frightened as he appeared to me like a roaring lion. We shared the rented flat with another couple, so he put his hand over my mouth to stifle my screams, as he did not want them to hear. I was at a loss to understand why Kumar suddenly started to beat me. Up until then, although ours was not a love match, we had been enjoying a peaceful companionship.

"From now on," he shouted, "you must have nothing to do with your parents!"

From that day, he continued to hit me whenever he lost his temper. He refused to take me to visit my parents or even give me a stamp so I could write to them. I concluded that he had become incensed with jealousy at seeing me so happy with my parents and family. In contrast, his home life had been very unhappy and our display of family love and unity might have struck a deep chord of resentment within him.

During the last month of my pregnancy my

husband was compelled to lift his ban on seeing my parents as, according to Hindu custom, he had to take me to stay with them for the confinement. My mother was with me when I gave birth to my daughter, Kanchana, in hospital on 31 August 1959.

I had to spend 30 days after the baby was born in one room of my parents' home. I was overjoyed at the opportunity to escape from Kumar's evil tyranny, and my parents were equally pleased to be able to see me after our enforced separation, although they were unaware of my sufferings.

During the period of confinement I was kept separate from the rest of the household, and my mother cooked and served my meals in my room. Today, they are not so strict and the nursing mother is just kept from going into the prayer room. I had to bathe in water mixed with special herbs and leaves. On the 31st day I was allowed to go to the temple to dedicate the baby with all the family when the priest performed the puja before the gods.

Forty days after the birth, with great trepidation, I returned to Vavuniya with Kumar and baby Kanchana. My mother was able to find a young servant girl, Manni, to help me care for the baby.

CHAPTER 4

Escape

I was seventeen years old when Kanchana was born. I now had someone to love and cherish in my misery. Kumar was transferred to a medical centre in Karaveddi, about 25 miles from my parents' home, but still in the country. We moved there to a small, L-shaped house consisting of three rooms and a kitchen with a verandah running along two sides. We used one of the verandahs as a dining area. It was luxury compared to the tiny flat at Vavuniya.

My mother had given me a dowry at the time of my marriage, consisting of jewellery and part of the house she owned, which would pass to me on her death. The other half of the house was owned by my mother's sister. When we moved to Karaveddi, Kumar sold the part of the house which my mother had given me, forcing me to sign the deeds as the house was in my name. My parents were living in the house at the time. Although they could have lived there for the rest of their lifetime, they were deeply hurt that I had sold the house, and chose to move out to rented accommodation.

After owning so much land and property and giving so much to their children, they found this a very demeaning experience and my father became ill for a while. It was a sad day for them to leave their home which originally belonged to my great-grandmother, and had been built in the early 1900s. At the time, my husband assured me that my parents were still living in the house and I did not learn the truth until about a year afterwards.

Kumar's cruel beatings became more and more unbearable. Every day after lunch he would have an hour's siesta. During this time I had to keep everything quiet. I was terrified that some slight sound might awaken the sleeping giant.

If a dog barked and woke him he would immediately fly into an uncontrollable rage. He would blame me and use a thick stick taken from a deck chair to mercilessly beat me. My arms, thighs and back became a mass of large bruises.

Every night before he went to sleep he would place a wooden bar across the door and push a table against it, piling buckets and basins on top. In this way he made sure that I would not be able to escape during the night without waking him from his sleep. He would also place a garden spade and a chopper under the bed and threatened to kill me and chop me up and nail me in a coffin.

To prevent me escaping during the day, he would bury broken glass in the patch of earth in front of the garden gate. At one time he was beating me so much that I ran to the store room and grabbed a bottle of Dettol. I was just about to drink some to end my misery, when he came up from behind and snatched the bottle away. I waited for the inevitable beating, but he walked away, thoughtful and subdued.

Although I longed to escape and make a life for myself and my baby, it all seemed so hopeless. I gradually lost all desire to resist and yielded to my husband's ruthless beatings day in and day out. I had lost all belief in any kind of God who had allowed the sufferings I continually endured.

One night as I tried to sleep, I felt Kumar's hands around my throat. As his grip tightened I struggled to free myself from beneath him, but he had both my hands pinned down beneath his knees as he crouched over me. I gradually became limp and gave up my struggle for life. It was then that I thought of my one-year-old baby, lying in the cot next to the bed. In a state of complete weakness I cried in my heart, "If there is a God please save me for the sake of my baby!"

At that moment there was a knock on the door. Kumar loosened his grip and went to answer it. I could hear muffled voices. I heard the front door shut and held my breath, my eyes tight shut. My heart was pounding fast as I lay still, not daring to move as I heard my husband approaching the bed. I felt the bed shake as he lay down beside me.

"It was a man asking the way. You escaped this

time," he snarled. "But don't think you have escaped forever. I will kill you with my own hands and put your body in the coffin and drive the nails into the box myself!"

I did not dare to let him hear me cry. They were tears of immense relief. Yet at the time, I did not realise that God had miraculously intervened.

My husband's sisters, Kunchu who was sixteen and Thevi who was fourteen years old, came to stay with us during their holidays from boarding school. They, as well as Manni the nine-year-old maid, were subjected to the same cruelty as myself. Kumar's violence knew no bounds.

In April 1961 when Kanchana was one year and eight months old, my younger brother, Pathmanathan, came to visit. Earlier that day, before my brother arrived, I had been badly beaten and my right ear was bleeding.

I had been sitting down when Kumar approached me from behind and punched my ear, but I was too frightened to tell my brother anything. I learned afterwards that my sisters-in-law had told Pathmanathan what had been happening. He stayed overnight, sleeping on the outside verandah. During the night, Kumar beat me relentlessly, but I would not utter a sound. I did not want my brother to hear, as Kumar had threatened that if I ever told my parents that he beat me he would not only kill me but them as well.

Unbeknown to me, however, Pathmanathan

watched everything through the window from the verandah. He was so upset but did not know what to do.

The next morning he left without breakfast and went straight home to tell my parents what was happening to me. My mother was distraught and came to see me the next day. I was so pleased to see her but did not tell her a thing, and she in turn did not utter a word of what she knew. My husband was so shocked to see her that he took a week off from work to be on hand and ensure I did not tell my mother anything.

Kumar's behaviour was immediately transformed for my mother's benefit. He treated me like a queen. That frightened me more than ever, for I knew that when my mother went home I would receive a "double portion" of beatings.

A week later on Friday evening when my mother was taking a shower, I was sitting on the verandah step feeding Kanchana when suddenly I felt an agonising blow in the middle of my back. I screamed and looked round to find Kumar brandishing a heavy torch, his eyes blazing with anger as he screamed, "Where is my dinner?"

Trembling and in intense pain, I went onto the verandah and lifted the large basket cover from the table, revealing the supper which my mother had prepared. With my baby cradled in my left arm, I went to hang the cover on the wall. Suddenly, Kumar grasped my shoulders and pulled me around to face him, pushing me hard against the wall. His eyes were ablaze and his face hideously contorted in crazed fury. I remember seeing his fist fly towards me and then a wild explosion of searing pain in my right eye. I screamed for my mother. She immediately came running from the shower wrapped in a sari with a towel on her head.

"What is happening?" she cried.

Kumar immediately became subdued, took the baby from me and lay on a deck chair saying nothing.

When my mother saw my face swollen black and blue and my eye puffed out of all proportion, she yelled at my husband, "Tell me, what has my daughter done to deserve such punishment?"

Kumar had no explanation and could only mutter nonsensically, "You've come to feed your baby have you?" as my mother continued to shout at him.

Night time came around and nobody wanted anything to eat. We went to bed, and with much fear and trepidation I had to sleep with my husband. My mother, sisters-in-law and the servant girl stayed helplessly outside the bedroom on the verandah unable to sleep. My mother had not asked me anything in front of Kumar, but that night she was able to glean all the information about my treatment from Kunchu and Thevi.

The next morning when I woke up I found that my mother had disappeared. Neither Thevi, Kunchu nor Manni knew where she had gone. I felt suddenly alone and fearful, but of course, Kumar was relieved that she had left. We had our breakfast and Kumar was getting ready for work when my mother suddenly reappeared.

"Where have you been?" I cried, relieved to have her back.

"I can go out, can't I?" was her mysterious reply.

Now Kumar was really worried. He could not understand what was going on and did not dare to ask. He called me into the bedroom. I followed trembling and fearfully wondering what he would do next.

He was agitated but his temper remained under control, his voice low.

"I have to go to work as I have already taken a week off. All because of you I might lose my job," he hissed. "I will go and sign off for another week, then come straight back. You must not say a word to your mother about what has been happening. If you do, I will kill you and your mother and everyone in the house."

I began to tremble and hastily assured him that I would not talk to my mother about anything. I did not mind dying, but I would not cause the death of my mother and the others. Yet I longed to fly into my mother's arms for comfort, but I knew I could not confide in her. I innocently believed that she had just come on a normal family visit, and was unaware that my brother had discovered the truth and had told her of my predicament.

That afternoon, as soon as Kumar went out, my

mother went to the next door neighbours and asked them to hire a car for us as quickly as possible. Shortly afterwards the car arrived and my mother said, "Pick up your baby and get into the car, we haven't a moment to lose."

I panicked and cried, "Where are we going?"

"I am not going to leave you here; you are coming home with me," she cried.

"But if we go, Kumar will come after us and kill us all. I do not mind dying, but I don't want you all to die because of me," I screamed.

"No one is going to die. I am taking you home and we will go to the police. You have nothing to worry about," she insisted, taking full charge of the situation.

Thevi, Kunchu and Manni begged us not to leave them behind, so my mother let them come as well. We gave the door key to the next-door neighbour and left without even stopping to pack. Throughout the two-hour journey to Sandirupay my mind was in turmoil. Although I was relieved to escape from my husband's clutches, I was terrified of the consequences and how Kumar might react. For the time being at any rate I could rest in the knowledge that he would be unable to follow us immediately, for at that time there was a curfew between 6 p.m. and 6 a.m., as there were civil riots throughout the region.

During the journey my mother told me what had happened when she had disappeared that morning. She had gone into the town to send a telegram to my father. Although it was early in the morning, the market was already crowded and my mother asked a lady who was passing if she could direct her to the post office. They fell into conversation and my mother discovered that the lady was my next-door neighbour.

"Do you mean to say that you are Kamala's mother and you allow her to suffer such cruelty?" said the neighbour. "Her husband beats her night and day and we hear her screaming out in pain! Why do you let this go on?"

"But I only heard about her plight last week and I came immediately," my mother insisted.

"You must take her home as soon as you can while she is still alive," my neighbour advised.

My mother hurried to the post office and sent a telegram to my father. She waited in vain for a reply. Apparently, my father had been out with friends during the day and had only found the telegram that evening when he reached home. He had been so worried and frustrated as he could do nothing because of the curfew. When we came through the door early that evening he was overwhelmed with relief, which soon turned to horror as we told him what had happened.

My parents' rented house was divided into two and was shared with their neighbour. It was shaped like our original home with a square courtyard in the centre which was divided in two by a fence. The following morning, the next-door neighbour called to us over the fence: "You have a visitor. I have seen your son-in-law coming down the path. Quickly, I will hide your daughter!"

I took the baby, and Thevi, Kunchu and Manni followed me into the neighbours' garden and through their back entrance. I kept imagining Kumar at my heels with his evil, grinning face, as I ran through the house. The neighbour led us into her bedroom. We dragged the bed against the door and I hid trembling beneath, with Kanchana clutched in my arms. I was petrified as I expected Kumar to burst into the room at any moment. I could hear the distant voices of my mother and Kumar arguing outside on the doorstep. Then the front door banged shut and Kumar's footsteps crunched back down the path. I held my breath, thinking that at any moment he would bang on the neighbours' door, but all was silent.

I breathed a sigh of relief when I heard my mother calling over the back fence, "He has gone, you can come out now." We thanked the neighbour profusely for her kindness in protecting us.

My mother was a paragon of strength and had refused to let Kumar into the house. Afterwards, I went with her to the police station and took out an injunction against Kumar to prevent him entering the house. Although he was unable to visit, he sent his friends and relations to plead with me to go back with him, but I would not relent.

Kumar wanted to take his sisters back and by law, we were not allowed to keep them, so had to release them into his custody. We immediately sent a telegram to Kumar's brother asking him to rescue them. Later, I was relieved to learn that he was able to take the sisters back to their boarding school, but not before they had suffered yet more cruelty from Kumar's hands. The servant girl returned to her parents and safety.

After the injunction had been imposed on Kumar, I was able to relax and slept day and night for nearly a week. I can only remember my mother waking me up at intervals to gently persuade me to have some food and drink. During that time, I was oblivious to all that was going on around me. My mother took care of the baby. I have vague recollections of my father being in tears most of the time, hugging and kissing me and saying how sorry he was for forcing me to marry such a man.

As time went on, I became a prisoner in my parents' home since I could not go out for fear of meeting my husband. I directed all my bitterness and anger towards my parents, blaming them for my predicament. I felt depressed and desolate, hopeless and helpless as I continued to hide from my husband.

I had nightmares and would wake up thinking he was there. We filed for divorce, but it would not come through until after we had been separated for seven years. I was continually looking over my shoulder expecting him to be there, waiting to drag me back to my previous agonising existence.

CHAPTER 5

Romance

I continued to have nightmares, bad dreams and panic attacks. I was filled with frustration and anger, yet I resolved in my heart to do my best for my child. My relatives were sympathetic and suggested that I consider a second marriage. The thought of another marriage repulsed me and brought new fears. What if my child's stepfather reacted badly to my daughter and brought more trauma upon us?

My past experiences had bred a deep, inward fear of embarking on any new relationship. Also, Kanchana had suffered enough in her early years. Even when she was a toddler she would cry in her baby language, "Daddy hit Mummy with his hands, with the stick and his legs." There were so many traumatic memories to eradicate from her mind. I did not want to add any more and totally rejected the idea of another marriage.

After a few months, my sister suggested we move

closer to her, and she arranged for Kanchana and myself and my parents to move into rented accommodation in Tellipalai, the village where my father was born. We lived amongst relatives, and a distant relative who was a Christian suggested I would feel better if I went to work and occupied my mind.

She arranged an interview for a job in a maternity hospital, the McLeod Hospital in Innuvil, Jaffna, which was once an American mission hospital. I was employed as a trainee dispenser of medicines and learned several other jobs. These included clerical work, switchboard operator, cashier, storekeeper, seamstress, linen storekeeper and catering superviser in rotation when the need arose. 'Jack of all trades' they called me, 'and master of none'!

I have many wonderful memories of working at the McLeod Hospital from 1961 until 1970. I began to feel independent and confident and was able to enjoy a social life. It was indeed a new life, a step in the right direction. I lived at the nurses' hostel as I did not want to travel alone on the bus for fear of meeting my husband. My daughter, who was then three years old, stayed with my parents and I visited her every week. Sometimes my father brought her over to spend time with me, which we both enjoyed so much.

I had my own room and ate my meals in the canteen. I made many friends among the nurses who lived at the hostel. Sometimes a group of us would go to the local cinema and I enjoyed singing the songs from the musicals. At other times we would sit in the garden in the cool of the evening and just talk. I was well known as a comedienne and used to make up stories to make them laugh.

Most of the nurses were unmarried, but dreamed of romance and marriage. Some of the older women had not married but were dedicated to their work. The doctors lived in bungalows within the hospital grounds and we would often baby-sit for them. I used to borrow books from them, mainly detective and romantic novels.

One day it seemed that I had stepped right into a chapter from one of those romances. I was working in the storeroom and the door suddenly opened. As I glanced up I found myself gazing into the large brown eyes of a handsome, smartly dressed rep. It was as if an electric shock pulsated through my whole being. I had never felt like this before. I was 21 years old and in love for the very first time. The immediate attraction was mutual. I was so excited and so very happy. I thought that maybe God had been kind enough to lead me to this person and was compensating me for what I had missed in life.

We talked on the telephone as it was not possible to meet with each other in public, for I was still waiting for the divorce to go through. Sam, a very good friend at work, offered his home as our meeting place. His wife willingly offered us hospitality. My happiness radiated in the workplace and soon a few of my friends were let into the secret of my involvement with JP. I invited him to meet my parents who were so delighted for me.

Three years passed and I was hoping that my divorce would soon come through so we could be married. All my previous fears of re-marrying had dissipated in the overwhelming love I felt for JP. He knew all about my past. Although I had not become a fully committed Christian, I felt that JP was God's gift to me. He was a Roman Catholic and very religious and we often spoke of spiritual things.

One afternoon, I went to visit a friend. She took out her photograph album and started to show me pictures of her friends and relations. Suddenly, one of the photographs seemed to leap out at me. It depicted a wedding group and the bridegroom was unmistakably JP! It was as if a knife had plunged into my heart. I had to stifle my tears and somehow find the words to calmly ask my friend, "Who are the couple getting married?"

"Oh, they are some friends I once knew in Colombo," she replied.

"I am sure I know these people. Could I borrow the photograph and have a copy made?" I asked.

"Of course," she said.

I took the photograph and had a copy made right away and returned the original to my friend.

I spent quite a few sleepless nights crying and asking God why He had done this to me. Again, I blamed God for my misfortunes and was not aware of the cunning works of the devil and the temptation he can put in our way. In my weakness I had yielded.

JP rang and I managed to chat with him as usual and asked him to meet me at Sam's. He said that he would love to come. I had a plan and prayed for courage and strength to carry it through. I took a taxi to Sam's and asked the driver to wait. Normally, JP would arrive late and I would always be on time. That fateful day, I was deliberately late and found JP had already arrived.

"He has been waiting about an hour," Sam told me before leaving us on our own.

"I have brought you a present JP," I said and handed him an envelope with the photograph in it.

I watched his face closely as he opened it. His expression was a mixture of shock and puzzlement.

"Where did you get this?" he asked.

"It doesn't matter how I came by it. I want you to please explain!" I replied.

Without hesitation he said, "This is my twin brother."

I was not impressed. "We have known each other for three years and you have never spoken about a twin brother. Who are you kidding?" I cried. "You have taken me for a fool. I wanted to see you to say goodbye. Please don't ever get in touch with me again."

With that I turned and walked out of the house. He came after me and pleaded, "Please don't go. I can explain. Please listen to me. I really do love you.

I never meant to cheat on you. I am separated from my wife just like you are from your husband."

"Then why didn't you tell me?"

He reached out to grasp my arm, but I pulled away, my heart beating fast and tears welled up in my eyes as I kept on walking. JP stopped me at the gate and fell on his knees declaring his love for me. Unheeding, I ran and got into the taxi. The taxi moved off and I cried all the way home and throughout that night.

Later, Sam told me that JP cried and begged to see me to explain, to say how sorry he was that I was hurt and how he wanted to make it up. But it was too late. He had had plenty of time to tell me of his situation, but now I could no longer believe what he said. All trust had gone and the old fears and insecurities flooded back. I was adamant that I never wanted to see him again, and kept my word. As far as I was concerned it had been true love and his memory was with me for many years.

CHAPTER 6

Transition

I felt broken and empty and once more resigned myself to the inevitability of remaining single. My only relief was the satisfaction of giving myself to Kanchana's upbringing and immersing myself in hospital life.

Our business manager's office was right opposite the dispensary. One day he heard so much laughter coming from the dispensary that he came in to see what was happening. Immediately he appeared in the doorway everyone became quiet and watched him stride towards me.

"What's going on?" he asked.

I boldly shared our joke and he went into fits of laughter. Although outwardly he was very authoritative, underneath he was really very soft and would often join in our mirth. He knew about my troubled past and whenever my daughter came to visit he allowed her to stay close to me while I worked

When my dad brought Kanchana on her visits my mother would send along a food parcel which I was able to share with my friends. One day my father left a parcel in the dispensary. I was on my break at the time and when I came into the dispensary all the staff were laughing.

"What's the joke?" I asked.

"Oh, Kamala," said one of the nurses. "Your father left the food parcel as usual, but the manager came in and opened it. When he saw 6-8 pieces of fried fish he said, 'Is she really going to eat all that?' "

Ever since then he called me "fatty". It sounds rude, I know, but he really was not rude at all but very kind. Knowing I would not travel by bus for fear of meeting my husband, he always let me use hospital transport with a driver provided.

At Christmas the hospital wards were all decorated and the best one was awarded a prize. Although it was a private hospital, two wards were allocated for the poor, who were given free treatment, and at Christmas the hospital management bought them presents.

The manager entrusted me with the responsibility of making the Christmas arrangements, which included buying the presents for the poor. I used to gather a few girls and put on a play in which I also took part. People from surrounding villages, schools and colleges would always attend. I made up original jokes which I would act out and everyone would fall about laughing. The only drawback was that whenever I went out with my friends, people would instantly recognise me. This caused me a great deal of embarrassment as I usually played a male character! Performing in public was not new to me, for when I was seven years old my mother arranged for me to take lessons in oriental dancing and singing. I often performed at school with other children until I was about thirteen.

Once, when my daughter came to visit me, I discovered she had a chest infection. She was admitted into the hospital and given antibiotic injections. When she was better the doctor said that she could go home. Kanchana was dismayed at the thought of leaving and suddenly had an "unexplainable" fit of coughing.

The doctor looked down at her with a smile and said, "Well, I think you can stay another two days."

She was really ecstatic and her cough miraculously disappeared!

One day a young woman with a little boy came into the hospital. She said that her husband had ill-treated her and she had nowhere to go. I felt an immediate empathy with her, so I went to the manager and begged him to give her a job in the hospital kitchen. He agreed to give her a trial and provided a room for her as well.

She used to wash my clothes and cook for me. I sometimes took her home with me at weekends, and her little boy and Kanchana enjoyed playing together. She later revealed that she was carrying another child, and when the baby was born I took a week off to look after her and bought things for the new baby. Eventually she decided to leave with her two children and go back to her husband. She kept in contact for a while, but when my life took a new direction we lost touch. The happiest years of my life were those spent at the McLeod Hospital. Those memories will always stay with me.

When Kanchana reached the age of six she started school at Union College, Tellipalai. She still remained at my parents' home and I visited her each week on my day off. During my visit I would call to see my sister who lived around the corner. I remember sitting quietly chatting to my sister when suddenly her daughter, Nalayini, ran excitedly into the room. Her dark eyes were wide with apprehension and her words tumbled out incoherently.

"Whatever is the matter?" I asked. "Slow down and tell us clearly what's wrong."

"It's Kanchana. I saw her daddy holding her hand and walking towards the school gates."

"No, you must be mistaken," I said, but my heart had already taken an uncontrollable leap. What I had feared had now finally happened. Kumar had taken Kanchana from me. My mind was plunged into turmoil. "I must go to the post office and phone the police," I said in a desperate effort to take charge of the situation.

Nalayini grabbed my hand and said, "I ran and told the headmaster what I had seen, and when I saw him walking towards Kumar at the gate I ran home to tell you."

That gave me a little hope that the head had intervened. I was just about to leave for the post office when Kanchana appeared in the doorway. Tears of joy and relief cascaded down my cheeks as I gathered her in my arms.

"What happened?" I cried.

"Daddy came to ask the teacher to let me go with him. He held my hand and walked out with me to the gate. I wasn't sure what was going to happen and was very frightened. He said he was going to buy me some sweets. I saw Nalayini in the distance but she ran away. Just before we reached the gates the headmaster came out and started to talk to Daddy. Then the school bell rang and I asked Daddy to let me go and collect my books. He let go of my hand and I ran back to the classroom. I ran out across the playground and out of the small gate at the back and came the long way round past the railway station and past auntie's house. She called me inside and asked me why I was running so I told her. She gave me a cup of Ovaltine and brought me home."

"You were very brave, Kanchana. You did very well," I said, hugging her tight. Poor Kanchana. She was so frightened and still trembling. Afterwards, the school principal told us that Kumar had spoken to Kanchana's teacher promising that it would never happen again. However, I was not convinced. Shopkeepers near to the school assured us that they would keep a look-out for us. Nevertheless, I was panic stricken and feared for our future. I was so proud of Kanchana and relieved that she had returned safely to us. I became even more protective of my precious daughter. From that time, I ensured that she was escorted to school, sometimes by my father, my niece or her school friends.

Although I had gained confidence in my new life, I was still fearful of Kumar. I was taunted by many mystifying questions regarding my troubled past. Our Hindu doctrine maintains that our suffering in this life is fate. We suffer for the sins we committed in our previous life. Our life endures after death according to what kind of lives we lead on earth. If we are bad, we are reincarnated as either grass, weeds, worms, snakes, stone, humans or even devils. If we are good, it is believed that we change to the state of a monk, and then become an angelic being, eventually becoming one with God.

I wondered about my own fate and what I must have done to deserve such a life as I had so far endured. Why did I suffer? I could not think I had ever sinned. If I had sinned, then I deserved the suffering and punishment I was going through. "How can I know my future? How am I going to bring up my child? My parents are old. What if they die? Why was I ever born to such a life of suffering?" My questions remained unanswered.

There was a small chapel in the hospital. The bell rang at 8 a.m. each morning, when most of the staff would go to the chapel before they started work. I was curious, and went along to find out what went on. As I entered the chapel I was surprised by its simplicity.

There were no idols or elaborate embellishments that I had been used to in the Hindu temples; just a wooden cross on a table in the front and rows of wooden pews. Mrs Sivaguru, who I learned afterwards was a deaconess, stood in front of the table and led us in singing and reading from the Bible. I had never experienced corporate worship before as I was only used to praying on my own before the idols. Finding it a very pleasant way to pass a brief half-hour, I decided to return each day. On one occasion a priest from another church came to preach. I can still remember his words.

"Jesus loves you just the way you are," he said. "He can forgive your sins. He can be your friend and you can talk to him. He will always answer your prayers."

I sat up and listened. This was new. Forgiveness, friendship, answered prayers. Were such things possible? I knew in my heart that this was the kind of God I wanted. It sounded as though this Jesus might even answer my questions. There was only one way to find out — I would talk to him. Surely, if he loved me, he would listen and answer me.

I wasted no time. That evening after work, I went to my room, shut the door and pulled up a chair.

I said, "Jesus, please come and sit down. I have a lot of questions. Could you please listen? I want answers to all of them."

I sat opposite the chair and asked, "Why was I born? Why did I have to suffer so early in my life? What does the future hold for myself and my child? If you are alive, as they say you are, you can hear me I am sure."

As I began to question, I started to cry. I put my head on the chair and told him all that I had suffered. I cried until I sank wearily into bed exhausted from weeping. This became my regular routine, as I thought I had to keep on until he spoke to me.

My condition improved and I was beginning to feel a lot better as I continued to pour out my heart to my invisible friend. Mrs Sivaguru helped me in my new-found faith and encouraged me to keep attending chapel. She gave me a Bible which I started to read. At first I could not understand a word of it, but I continued to talk to Jesus my friend.

I felt that I had been allowed to grow up in my time at the McLeod Hospital. I experienced freedom, independence and safety, surrounded by so much love and friendship. Now, as I grew in faith and confidence and received inner healing from the Lord, I began to feel a real person again. I had become bubbly and outgoing, always making others happy.

CHAPTER 7

A new beginning

One night I had the most amazing dream. I was standing on a mountain amongst some other women whose heads were covered. We all had lighted candles in our hands. It was very dull and cloudy, yet I could see Jesus in the distance hanging on the cross. He cried out in a loud voice: "It is finished!" Immediately, everything went dark, our candles went out and someone in the crowd re-lit them. At that point I was given communion. I awoke from the dream, yet it was more than a dream. It was so vivid, and even now I can picture the scene just as plainly as I did then.

It is impossible to adequately describe what happened to me that morning. It was as if new blood surged through my body from my head to my feet. My heart was bursting with gladness and my feet hardly touched the floor as I walked. I felt as if I had been taken out of my dark pit of despair to a new place. Just as Jesus tasted the bitterness of the

vinegar and cried, "It is finished!", all the bitterness
of my sufferings had finished. He had taken them
upon Himself and in return had given me peace. I
could not stop talking about my wonderful dream.

Everything seemed to explode within me. I felt
no pain, no depression, no anxiety but an
enormous amount of love and forgiveness. It was
as if Jesus had wiped the slate clean. Even if I had
wanted to think about my sufferings, I could not. I
did not hurt any more. I forgave my father **and my
ex-husband**. I became a little wiser than before. It
was an unbelievable transformation.

It was years later, in the mid-eighties when I
read Mark 15: 40. I was awestruck to discover how
the scene described the women looking on afar off,
just as it had been in my dream. (The words, "It is
finished" are recorded by John, Chapter 19: 30.) I
marvel at the truth of God's Word and how He
made it so real to me that day.

I went on talking to God as if to a friend and I
asked Him what the future held for me. Again God
spoke to me in a dream. I saw a large expanse of
water. A very old man with curly hair, dressed in a
white robe with a stick in his hand, was walking
towards the water and I followed him. He silently
pointed to the water with his stick. He gave no
verbal instructions but clearly intimated that I was
to go through the water. As I stepped into the
water, I awoke from my dream. I shared this dream
with my friends and they said they thought God

was showing me that I would be going abroad. This seemed impossible as I did not have enough money to travel and the thought of going abroad had never entered my head.

Shortly afterwards, I had another dream. This time, I came to a place of trees with no leaves. The atmosphere was very smoky and when I came out from among the trees, I saw Dr Sethurajan, standing there with her little boy beside her. She had previously worked at the McLeod Hospital and I did some baby-sitting for her. She went to America and then England to further her medical training. It was in England that she married Uncle Sethurajan and lived and worked as a paediatric doctor.

Not long after my dream, I received a letter from her asking me to go to England. She knew all about my sufferings and asked me if I would help her as she was expecting her second baby. If I agreed, she would send me a ticket so that I could join her as soon as possible. I was so excited and shared the news with my parents.

My father said, "You can't go too far away from us. We will never see you again."

But I was determined to take advantage of the opportunity. My aunt had said that I could stay with her for two or three years and train to become a nurse. She suggested my daughter could follow me and be educated in England. In this way I would be better able to provide for my daughter.

It would be difficult to part with Kanchana, but

the prospect of her joining me made it easier. I asked her, "Will it be all right if I go to England for a while?"

"Yes, of course," she replied.

"You realise I will not be able to come home at weekends to see you as I do now."

"It will be all right," she insisted.

I accepted my aunt's offer and she sent me a ticket immediately. I set out for England in June 1970. Saying goodbye to my daughter and my parents in Jaffna before leaving for the airport was so painful, especially leaving Kanchana. She was almost eleven years old and I did not know how long it would be before I could see her again.

Also, I still feared for her safety, even though, after waiting seven years, my divorce application had gone before the courts and I had been granted the Decree Absolute in January of that year. I worried that my husband might try to kidnap her once I was gone. But my mother and father assured me that she would be safe and that they and all the family and friends would be watchful.

I was comforted to know that I was leaving her in safe and loving hands. I felt a keen sense of Jesus calling me away across the sea to make a new life, not only for me but also Kanchana when I was able to finance her journey to England and support her. It was a new adventure, yet tinged with apprehension as I faced an unknown future, but I was determined to trust in Jesus each step of the way.

My brothers saw me off at the airport in Colombo and I travelled on a new Boeing 747 jumbo jet. As it soared into the air I felt a thrill of excitement, all sadness dissipating in a wave of joy and expectancy as I set out on a new life with the Lord, far away from Kumar's pursuing footsteps. Yet at the same time, I was aware of being suddenly alone and separated from my daughter and my family.

The plane landed en route in Bombay where I spent the night at the Taj Mahal Hotel. It was very grand and I was treated like a VIP. The airline had arranged for a taxi to take me to the hotel. As the taxi drew up to the door, a porter held an umbrella over my head and, although I was a little embarrassed, I felt like a queen.

A lift whisked me up several floors to my room. I gazed in wonder at the beautiful, softly lit room, at the comfortable bed with luscious soft covers and writing desk on the opposite wall. I walked across the shiny marble floor to the luxurious en suite bathroom. I ran my hand over the soft towels and gazed into the shining mirror above the wash basin. There in front of me was something I had never seen before — a shiny hot water tap! I was soon treating myself to a hot bath. Clean and fragrant after luxuriating in the hot suds, I made use of the writing desk and wrote a letter to my parents.

When I had finished writing there was a soft

knock on the door. I couldn't think who it could be. I opened the door to find a gentleman from the room next door. He invited me to have dinner with him. At first I was a little apprehensive to accept the offer of a stranger, but as I did not know my way around, I decided to chance it. He was very charming and his polite, easy manner immediately put me at my ease. I was so grateful to have him escort me as I gingerly set foot on the slippery tiled floor of the dining room. The enormous room was dotted with small tables, beautifully set with candles and gleaming cutlery. An orchestra was quietly playing. This was a far cry from my village existence and was all so new to me.

I was thrilled to sample the luxury of air travel once more as I continued my journey the next day. As the plane touched down at Heathrow Airport, I gathered my belongings together, my inside churning with excitement. When I emerged from the plane and began the long walk to retrieve my luggage, I felt a distinct chill in the air.

My uncle and aunt welcomed me in the arrival lounge and my aunt placed a coat around my shoulders. I was unaccustomed to the weight pulling on my shoulders as we walked towards the family car which would take us to their flat in Shepherds Bush.

When we reached London the buildings seemed so enormous, towering above me and I was overwhelmed by the number of cars and crowds of people. It was so different from the quiet beauty of the country I had left behind. The reddish brown earth and scrub had been replaced by an arid concrete jungle which stretched all around me. My heart ached for my homeland and loved ones, yet I was determined to carve out a new life to ultimately share with my daughter in the coming years.

Having reached the flat, we had lunch. Afterwards I saw television for the first time and could not stop looking at it. The conditions were very cramped and I slept in the lounge on a sofa bed. There was only one lounge and one bedroom and a small kitchen with room enough for only one person at a time. Later, we moved to a large house with four bedrooms where I had my own bedroom to share with baby Shantha who was two months old.

As I witnessed the four seasons come and go, I marvelled at their beauty. I trod the sun-baked pavements of the City in summer and enjoyed walking through the park ablaze with so many colourful flowers. I revelled in the rich colours of autumn. But spring was especially exhilarating, with new life bursting from the plants and trees and the fresh, warm breeze contrasting with the sharp cold winds of winter which I found difficult to endure.

I remember looking out of the window at the trees with no leaves and the fog. It was then I recalled my dream of the leafless trees and recognised that the smoky atmosphere was actually fog. It was awesome to realise how God had answered my questions about my future through that dream and placed me just where He wanted me.

Later, out of the same window one dank winter's day I cried, "What are all those insects flying in the air? There are thousands of them!"

"They are not insects," said my uncle. "It is snowing!"

I looked closer at the myriad white bodies falling thick and fast and was relieved and fascinated to realise that they were soft flakes of snow falling silently on the rooftops. I had never seen such a spectacle before and gazed in wonder at the thickening carpet of snow accumulating on the street below.

Since leaving for England I had had so many new and exciting experiences which alleviated my sadness. I missed Kanchana so much and she also began to pine. We wrote to each other frequently, which eased the pain and I was always looking for the postman to hear news of my daughter. Although my prayers had been answered and I had been given a new beginning, I found it difficult to adjust.

Life in my new environment involved hardships, demanding perseverance with patience, tolerance with tears, overcoming language difficulties and adapting to strange ways. Yet my aunt and uncle helped me so much to adjust and conform to a new pattern of living. As well as looking after baby Shantha I also cared for his three-year-old brother, Raj. They brought me a lot of comfort and consolation.

I took a job in the evenings cleaning the offices of an engineering firm. My uncle and aunt thought it would give me confidence to go out and meet people and that I would benefit from work experience.

Saturday was my day off and I would make a hot flask of tea, pack up some sandwiches and head for Shepherds Bush library. There I enjoyed reading Shakespeare and other classical literature as part of a postal course in English which I had undertaken. At last I would be able to catch up on my education. As I journeyed to the library each Saturday morning, I watched hordes of people rushing to and fro and listened to the underground trains thundering past and thought, "Where is everyone going?" Caught up in the crush of the crowds, I wondered what was going on.

When I travelled on the train I would become very embarrassed to see couples kissing and cuddling in public. This was all strange to me and people were actually eating on the train. Why did they do this? Why didn't they do these things in the privacy of their own home? I would listen carefully to people's conversations and ask my uncle many questions. He patiently dealt with all my queries, helping me to understand the Western way of life and I also learned a lot from watching television.

Each night I continued my studies into the early hours of the next morning. I spoke a little textbook English, practising with a Sunday School teacher in the Methodist Church which I attended with my aunt. But I needed to become more proficient. Though painfully arduous, I found my studies both satisfying and fulfilling and, with hindsight, I can see God's hand in this training. His grace never departed from me and gave me strength to continue.

After staying two and a half years with my uncle and aunt, I applied to Orsett Hospital near Grays in Essex to train as a nurse. As I lacked the basic educational qualifications when I applied, the School of Nursing wanted to test my proficiency in English before deciding to take me on.

They asked me to write an essay on the subject of parents staying with their children in hospital. At that time it was not accepted practice. I had been very upset when Shantha had been admitted into Great Ormond Street Hospital, for I had to leave him with tears rolling down his face as he spread out his arms, imploring me not to leave him. From this experience, I was able to write the essay straight from my heart.

The Principal summoned me to his office and I went along the corridor thinking, "Oh, I know I'm not going to get the job."

I stood trembling in front of his desk.

"I am very impressed with your essay and the standard of English. How long have you been in this country?" he asked.

"Two and a half years," I replied.

"I could never write so well in your language after being in your country for such a short time," he said with a warm smile.

I told him how I had taken a postal course in English and taught myself by reading books from the library.

He was so impressed that he immediately offered to take me on to train as a nurse. I was so amazed to hear his words of commendation. This was a great achievement indeed and I owe it all to the grace of God alone. Yet I am also grateful to my uncle and aunt for their help and support in making it all possible.

I moved to Orsett in March 1973 to commence my two years SEN training at Orsett Hospital. By God's grace I excelled in my class and became the best pupil with a certificate to prove it! To my shame, I claimed all the credit, but have since realised that God was granting me the ability. It was He who enabled me to even speak the language. I qualified in May 1975.

I enjoyed nursing and was very happy working at Orsett Hospital. Although it was very demanding it was also really challenging. I lived in the nurses' home adjacent to the hospital, and often in the evenings a few of us started to play badminton. We liked it so much that we decided to form a badminton club.

There were about 18-20 regular players and I was the elected chairperson. We arranged tournaments with other hospitals and bought trophies to present to the best players at special social functions which we arranged. The sport definitely kept me healthy and trim. I carried on playing for about ten years, until other responsibilities took precedence.

Learning different aspects of diseases, symptoms and treatments was very stimulating. Heart was my best subject. The experience of working in the heart unit inspired me to study more on my own. I borrowed books on medicine from the library and studied so much that my knowledge excelled, much to the amazement of my colleagues. However, I thank God that He gave me the strength and inspiration to study. Without Him I could not have succeeded.

I found work in the intensive care unit the most challenging. People were often admitted in a traumatic state with little chance of survival. Yet, with all the expertise of the doctors and nursing care and the aid of modern technology their recovery always proved such a joy. But it was so sad when someone died despite all our efforts. At such times the only rewarding aspect was to be with the relatives to comfort them, make cups of tea and cry with them.

Morag Waterman, a Christian lady, used to visit us in the nurses' home. She went on to start a Nurses' Christian Fellowship which met in her own home and sometimes at the large country house in Orsett belonging to Lord and Lady Whitmore. In this way, I was still drawn to Christianity and fellowship, but I did not attend church. Morag became a very dear friend and sister in Christ. I shall always cherish the experiences of my working life. Without God I would never have achieved so much. To Him be the glory forever.

CHAPTER 8

A closer walk

With new freedom, I had new friends who lived to please themselves. Where they went I followed, to the pub and disco dancing. I started to smoke like all the others and enjoyed what they enjoyed. Yielding to all the temptations and attractions in the world around me seemed so plausible to me. After all, having gone through so much suffering, didn't I deserve some enjoyment? Thus I convinced myself. Consequently, my actions brought me pain, disappointment, heartache and disillusionment. Unbeknown to me I had grieved the Lord, who had shown me such grace and loving kindness.

In my shame, I cried out for God's help. When I turned to Him, He was willing to forgive and forget my transgressions. *"Come now, and let us reason together,' says the Lord. 'Though your sins are like scarlet, they shall be as white as snow'."* (Isaiah 1:18).

I proved the truth of His word; He washed me and made me clean.

As well as working full-time at Orsett Hospital, I worked as an agency nurse in London on my days off and during my holidays. In this way, I was soon able to pay for Kanchana's airline ticket and, to my utmost joy, I was reunited with my daughter.

Just after she joined me in England, we celebrated her sixteenth birthday and started to live as mother and daughter after five years of separation. Not only had I saved enough money for Kanchana's fare, I was able to take her on a shopping trip to buy her some clothes and everything she needed. It gave me great delight to fill my cupboards and fridge with her favourite foods.

As Kanchana was not allowed to live at the nurses' home with me, Morag very kindly let her live in a room in her house for a while, but she would always visit me in the evening before returning to Morag's. After that, she went to stay with my cousin in Pitsea and travelled to Thurrock Technical College by bus. Soon, I was able to rent a room in the village of Horndon-on-the-Hill which was not far from the hospital. Kanchana was able to live with me there and cycle to college each day. In 1978 I was able to rent a two-bedroom council flat a few miles away in Grays.

Kanchana had to resit her O-Levels in English, going on to gain her Ordinary National Diploma. At about this time, much to our grief, we learned that

Kumar had committed suicide. Kumar's behaviour had been caused by schizophrenia and he had been taken into a mental hospital. There his aggressive behaviour continued. He even beat the carers and they had to tie him to the bed. Nevertheless, he escaped several times and on one occasion he went to his brother's office in Colombo and attacked him. It was during his last escape that he had died. When we heard the sad news, we wept bitterly and mourned the loss of a life which could have been so different. Even after his death, I still had the usual nightmares until my faith grew stronger.

Kanchana took a course in banking and, at the age of 19, started her first job in a bank. During this time, about a year after she had joined me in England, I booked a holiday to Sri Lanka. Just before I was due to leave, however, Kanchana became very sick with severe pains in her back. I took her to hospital where they admitted her for investigation. I was so very worried and went early the next morning to visit her.

As I approached her bed I was concerned to see that she looked very distraught. "Mum, just go and look in the toilet."

I was shocked to see the pan filled with blood and ran quickly to summon a nurse. She came running in and called for the doctor. He immediately sent Kanchana for X-rays, which confirmed that she had a problem with one of her kidneys, and they decided to operate the next day.

I was devastated. That night I was unable to sleep.

After being reunited with Kanchana for such a short space of time, I could not face the possibility of losing her. I had prayed earnestly that Kumar would not take her from me, surely the Lord would not allow her to be taken from me now! I can still feel the turbulent emotions I experienced during that traumatic time. I remember the endless wait in the hospital, the nurse coming towards me and my heart almost coming to a halt as I waited for her fateful words.

She smiled reassuringly, "The operation has been a complete success. They have removed the dysfunctional kidney and Kanchana will be fine."

I was so relieved and thanked God for his goodness in bringing her through and also for allowing the problem to be discovered before I left for Sri Lanka. I was able to transfer my ticket into my daughter's name and send her to Sri Lanka to convalesce.

In 1980, at the age of 75, my mother came to visit me. She was so delighted to come to England and took many photographs. She still treasures the photo album she compiled of her visit and shows it to all who come to see her. She was thrilled to see snow for the first time and the royal family when we visited Windsor and saw them en route to Ascot. I had cherished a desire to see the Queen since early childhood.

"I have been living in England for ten years and have never seen the Queen," I said. "Now you come and we see almost the entire royal family!"

"A-ah, I'm the lucky one!" she declared.

My mother was able to meet Thanesh, whom my daughter had married the previous year. It was a love match — as I was careful to ensure that she did not have to undergo an arranged marriage!

Kanchana gave birth to a baby boy in 1983 and named him Simon. Our delight was soon turned to a nightmare, however. The baby had difficulty in breathing. After a scan it was revealed that he had a trachea-oesophageal fistula, which meant that his windpipe and food pipe were stuck together. Consequently, he was unable to take his feed from either his mother or a bottle. Within hours of his birth he was rushed to the operating theatre.

Once more I had to endure a long, anxious wait, this time in the company of Kanchana and Thanesh. I prayed earnestly for this brand new life which was being threatened so soon. After surgery, the baby was transferred to the intensive care unit of the Queen Elizabeth Hospital in London. Here we continued our anxious wait, only to be told that they had discovered a large ventricular hole in his heart. He had to be fed via a tube inserted into his abdomen. When he started to swallow milk, the stomach tube was removed before sending him home with medication.. They intended to operate on his heart at a later date.

Instead of returning home jubilant with a new-born baby, we had to grapple with the problem of nursing him round the clock, 24 hours a day. Having given birth and then spending most of her time in hospital, Kanchana did not care about herself. She was so worried and upset about the child, so I thought it would really help her if she went to work after her maternity leave. In this way we would be able to share the responsibility. Kanchana and Thanesh worked from Monday to Friday and I worked at weekends so I could look after the baby during the week.

As the baby could not take milk from a bottle, we had to feed him with a pippet, then a syringe. He was on medication and regularly attended the outpatients department of the Queen Elizabeth Hospital. Baby Simon was eventually able to have his heart operation in Great Ormond Street Hospital when he was just eleven months old. He weighed only 11lb. Again we had to endure yet another anxious wait. The wait seemed endless. I prayed earnestly until I saw the doctor coming towards us. I searched his face but could read nothing there to give us an inkling of what had transpired.

When he reached us, his face immediately broke into a smile as he assured us that the operation had been a success. We were so relieved and thankful. But much to our horror, later in the evening the baby developed complications and had to be rushed back to theatre not once but twice in 48 hours. He was taken to the ITU and put on a life support machine, and we thought we would never see the baby again.

I continued to pray and plead with God. Kanchana joined me in prayer in the hospital chapel. It is impossible to put our feelings of anxiety and distress into words as we continued to pray. Tearful and anxious, we had once again to face the doctor. We trembled and almost dreaded to hear what he had to say, fearing the worst.

Once more he smiled and said, "Everything is fine. The baby has come through."

God graciously answered our prayers. Our tears were of relief. Baby Simon had survived the operations and began to show signs of improvement. Much to our joy, he was discharged from hospital. During his stay he had been very unhappy and cried for most of the time, but when we took him outside the ward he immediately stopped crying. He was home in time for his first birthday. My friend, Cathy, brought him a Humpty Dumpty. Simon had been put together again and we celebrated his safe deliverance!

From then on we looked after him and watched his progress closely. At first, we had to take him to the hospital for a check-up each week, then every two weeks. After this he needed only a monthly visit, then every three months and finally every six months. When he reached the age of thirteen he only had to visit the hospital once a year. Now, he only needs a check-up every three years and lives a normal, healthy life. We are so grateful to God. It was such a relief to my daughter and her husband who had undergone such a distressing time.

At the time, however, I could not see the hand of God. Whilst looking after the baby and working three nights a week, I had become very tired as I had lost so much sleep. My daughter and her husband, of course, were equally affected, if not more.

I had not realised this accumulation of fatigue was affecting not only my work but my faith in God. Everything seemed so dark and meaningless. I became very bitter and even denied the very existence of God, who had allowed us to go through such overwhelming anxiety. I remember crying out in anguish, "There is no God! If he does exist, why has he let this happen to my grandson?"

A Christian friend, Catherine Benton, whom I worked with at the time, heard my cries and was most concerned for me. Gently, she helped to restore my faith in God. I will never forget the goodness and grace of God in providing such an angel to help me through.

She told me later that on the first night she talked with me about the Lord, she was also going through a difficult time. That night she had prayed, "Lord, if you want me to continue working nights, could you show me someone who I can lead to the Lord?" God answered her prayer and she led me back to Him.

It was through this friend and her family that I fully committed my life to Christ. I was baptised in January 1984 by her husband David, (who later became a London City Missionary). What a friend we have in Jesus! In my journey I had once again deviated and struggled through dark, rough terrain, but the Lord led me back on to the right pathway once more and even closer to Himself.

My baptism in 1984

CHAPTER 9

The light of His presence

I attended church regularly with Catherine each Sunday. My daughter and her family had moved to Kent when Simon was two and a half years old, as Thanesh took a job in Erith. Two years later in 1986, much to our joy, baby James, a brother for Simon, was born.

Although I missed them very much, I concentrated on walking with God, reading my Bible regularly and attending Bible studies. I started to build up my spiritual learning. Peter, my next-door neighbour, was a Christian. He was such a kind, exuberant person and told me about the experience of the Baptism of the Holy Spirit. He often quoted the words of John the Baptist, "*I indeed baptise you with water unto repentance, but He who is coming after me is mightier than I, whose sandals I am not worthy to carry. He will baptise you with the Holy Spirit and fire.*" (Matthew 3: 11).

This was all new to me and at first I could not agree with Peter, yet inwardly I desired a deeper experience of the Holy Spirit.

In December 1986 I had a varicose vein operation and had to spend two weeks at home. During this time, I earnestly prayed for the Holy Spirit to fill me. I wept and cried out to God, confessing my sins. As I did so, I could see in my mind's eye a bottle of oil with sediment at the bottom. When the bottle was shaken the sediment floated to the top. Just like the sediment, my unconfessed sins were brought to the surface. ("... *the goodness of God leads you to repentance.*" Romans 2: 4b). One by one I confessed my sins and knew the deep joy of accepting His forgiveness.

Peter gave me two testimonial books, *I Dared to Call Him Father,* written by a Muslim lady who became a Christian, and *Journey to Jerusalem,* a book by Derek Prince about his wife's experience of the Holy Spirit's power in her life. I longed to experience the presence of God as did those I read about in the books. The yearning became an earnest prayer deep within me. I continued to pray, "Please come, Lord."

As I prayed, the Bible seemed to spring alive and a light was literally shining upon the words. I would go to bed thinking, "I hope the Lord does not come when I am asleep and I miss Him." So I would try to keep awake. I wanted to see Him so much and could think of nothing else.

My sick leave came to an end and I was due to

return to work. It was a Saturday evening and I called in to see Peter and his wife Rosemary. They were talking to me but I wasn't able to concentrate on what they were saying, as my innermost being was still seeking God. I politely excused myself and returned to my flat to get ready for work, quietly trying to console myself: "After all, He is God and may decide not to turn up at all. How could I expect God to come to me!"

As I walked into the lounge, I was quite taken aback to find the room bathed in a bright light. The presence of God was so powerful that I could not stand but fell upon my knees weeping. I felt unable to stand before His holiness as I was so unworthy and insignificant. It was awesome.

"Jesus," I cried. "How can you come to visit a sinner like me? You are the Lord Almighty who has created the universe!"

I prayed and cried out to Him. Then I heard His voice. I couldn't see Him, but heard Him say very clearly, "Love me".

I got up and looked around the flat which, in the brightness of God's presence, seemed so dusty and untidy. "How can the Lord visit me here?" I thought. My heart was beating so hard and fast it seemed as if two hearts were beating within me. I was so brimful with awe that I felt I had to share my experience with someone. So I ran next door to Peter and Rosemary.

"The Lord came!" I cried. "The Lord Jesus came!"

Peter asked, "Why are you crying? What

happened?"

"The Lord came to see me," I replied. "He came! He came! Oh, Peter it was so wonderful. He spoke to me and told me to love Him."

They were so delighted to hear this and cried out: "Hallelujah! Praise the Lord!"

I then had to rush to work. As I drove along and as I worked throughout the night, my whole being, spirit, soul and mind, was praising God. How I performed my duties throughout that night without making one single mistake I do not know.

When I returned home the next morning, I tried to sleep as I normally did after a night's work. I went to bed but couldn't settle as I felt so hot, although it was snowing outside. I threw off the bed cover, but still could not cool down. My skin was burning hot, so I thought I might have a temperature and put a thermometer into my mouth. My temperature was normal.

Again, I could not lie down as my whole being wanted to continually praise God. I got out of bed and went into the lounge and continued to praise and marvel at how God had appeared to me the previous day. What a wonderful God he was! I sat awestruck and couldn't sleep. I was not hungry or thirsty, yet I had so much energy and wanted to shout from the housetops, "Jesus Christ is Lord!"

Soon the next night came and I had to get ready for work. I went to work as before praising God in my heart, still making no mistakes and still feeling very hot.

I went to see Peter the next day. "I am so scared," I said. "I feel so hot, I can't sleep, yet I have so much energy. I feel as if I've touched a live wire and 5,000 volts of energy are pulsating through me."

Peter was at a loss to know what to do. He laid his hands upon me and prayed: "Whatever has happened to Kamala has made her so frightened and so hot. Please Lord, cool her down."

On the third night I went to work and when my colleague had gone for her break, I sat watching my patients in ITU. I prayed that God would cool me down, and as I prayed, I started to grow cooler. Then God caused me to look at myself from a distance. It was as if I was looking at myself for the first time. I will never forget what I saw: the ugliest, dirtiest, most horrid looking lump! I immediately prayed: "God, that is not me! Usually people tell me how good I am. How can this be me?"

The Lord said, "That is you, Kamala, for without me you are nothing. Do you still want me to cool you down?"

"Lord," I replied, "if that is me, I really do not want to cool down if it means I will be without You. Please make me warm again."

Gradually the heat came back. I realised that I had experienced the baptism of fire as mentioned in Matthew 3: 11, "*I indeed baptise you with water unto repentance, but He who is coming after me is mightier than I, whose sandals I am not worthy to* carry. *He will baptise you with the Holy Spirit and fire."* When I feel good about myself, I always remember that in the eyes of God I am not good at all. I am only what He makes me to be by His Holy Spirit. The glory goes to Him alone. *"I am the vine, you are the branches. He who abides in Me, and I in him, bears much fruit; for without Me you can do nothing"* (John 15: 5).

The following is an extract from a poem the Lord gave me at the time:

My Name is Abide in Him

My name is Abide in Him, my life is what I am.
I am what I am, because I was who I was.
I was who I was because I descended from sin.
My name was sin until He came to give me
A new life and a new name.
My name is Abide in Him, my life is what I am.

He who came, Him I crucified.
When I crucified, He cried, "Father forgive."
His Father, whose name is I AM WHO I AM,
Loved His Son, so heard His plea.
He forgave me and changed my name
My name is Abide in Him, my life is what I am.

My name is sin no more, but I am not sinless,
I am purged and cleansed.
I have a promise of hope to be perfect one day

When I see the One I crucified, who rose from the dead.
Then I will be His sister and daughter to His Father.
My name is Abide in Him, my life is what I am.

I have a new name, I have a new life, but still I have the old self!
How to die to the old self and put on a new self?
This wisdom I hold in the palm of my hand:
To put the old self on the cross and put on the new self
To live up to my new name.
My name is Abide in Him, my life is what I am.

The Lord was so real during this exciting time. After working during the night and still not able to sleep, I went into town to do some shopping. I was walking back to my car when God spoke to me in my heart so clearly: "Turn around and go back to the Christian bookshop."

I immediately turned and went back as the Lord directed. As I neared the shop the Lord told me that I would meet a friend and that I was to make her a gift of some money. I took a ten pound note from my bag and put it in my pocket in readiness. When I entered the shop, the very person the Lord had told me about was coming down the stairs followed by her husband.

I wondered how I could give her the money

without causing any embarrassment. I pretended to study the books on the shelves, as I struggled in my heart to know what to do next. As she walked towards me, my hand went immediately into my pocket and clutched at the note.

She looked very drawn as she greeted me and went on to confide that she was absolutely broke. She only had £1.50 to last her the rest of the week until pay day. Without hesitating, I took the crisp ten pound note from my pocket and thrust it into her hand.

"Are you sure you can spare all this?" she asked, her eyes wide in astonishment.

"Of course," I replied. "The Lord told me to give it to you."

She was so pleased and grateful. God had known her need and as I came out of the shop, I praised Him for giving me the privilege of sharing at a time of need.

That evening I prayed to God and asked Him to give me sleep. I had worked three nights without any food or sleep. I had the night off from work and had arranged to visit some friends at 6 o'clock. It was now 5 p.m., so I lay down on the sofa and asked the Lord to grant me sleep for half an hour. I immediately fell into a deep sleep and exactly 30 minutes later I awoke to find myself speaking in a different language. It came from the depths of my being in a torrent of strange unknown words. I thought, "I must write this down," and tried to memorise the words, but afterwards I could never recall them.

I went with Peter and his wife to visit friends and shared my experience with them. The time went so quickly and it was well past midnight when I left. Peter and Rosemary had left earlier. As I drove, I began to feel frightened because I knew that the lamp next to my garage at the back of the flats had not been working for the past two years, and I would be in total darkness. Often people would be hanging about in this area and as my headlights pierced the darkness I thought I could see dark forms lurking in the shadows.

I felt suddenly afraid and began to tremble and prayed for God's help. As I approached the garage I was amazed to find the lamp was on. I thanked and praised God that at last the council had repaired the lamp. The light shone right into the garage as I parked the car.

The following evening when I went to get into my car to go to work, the light outside the garage was out and still in its damaged state as it had been for years. God had provided me with light that previous evening! The lamp was not repaired until after the 1987 storm. It was yet another manifestation of God's wonderful presence during that memorable time.

Before I went to sleep that night I prayed, "Lord, I am so tired. I really need to sleep so much." The Lord granted my prayer and I slept solidly for ten hours.

When I woke up the next morning I could smell a

most beautiful fragrance.   "What could it be?" I wondered. I had not sprayed any air freshener, but the scent filled the whole flat.

I took a bath and as I was bathing the water looked crystal clear. I splashed and revelled in its purity. I felt washed and pure. As I got out of the bath it felt as if I was adorned in a white garment with a light above me. I dressed and walked into the lounge and praised God amidst the pervading fragrance.

Suddenly, there was a knock on the door. It was Peter, who asked me if I would like to borrow a cassette. I took the tape from him and immediately played it over. I was amazed to hear the song, "Take His hand you lovely Bride!" It was incredible. The Lord had prompted Peter to bring the tape which summed up my whole experience.

I was still praising God at 3 o'clock in the afternoon. I vacuumed the whole place through and placed candles in the windows to brighten the dark winter afternoon. Then, for the first time in three days, I felt suddenly hungry.

"I will lay the table for the Lord and myself," I thought.

I cooked a meal and set the table for two. As I sat with the food on my plate, I became aware of His presence opposite me across the table. In retrospect, I am reminded of the words in Revelation 3: 20, "*Behold, I stand at the door and knock. If anyone hears My voice and opens the door, I will come in to him and dine with him, and he with Me.*"

I was transfixed by an overwhelming feeling of

love enveloping me. I basked in His loving presence and it seemed as if time did not exist. I sat for what seemed hours, but it was in fact only five minutes. It was as if the Lord was saying, "This is how eternity will be — timeless." I thought, "I hope nobody disturbs this marvellous peace and stillness." In that moment the Lord's presence departed.

I looked for Him in every room but could not find Him. Even the fragrance had disappeared. ("*I opened for my beloved; but my beloved had turned away and was gone. My heart leaped up when he spoke. I sought him, but I could not find him; I called him, but he gave me no answer.*" Song of Solomon 5: 6).

I felt that my jealous guarding of the Lord's presence might have caused Him to leave. As I realised later, God's love is for all mankind, not just for me and I have no particular claim on Him for myself alone. After this experience, I had a greater understanding of the Word of God and Jesus became much more real. The Lord had revived my soul.

After seeking God earnestly, I had truly experienced the Baptism of the Holy Spirit. I would like to emphasise that I am not special or better than anyone else, but am grateful to God for such deep experiences of Himself.

CHAPTER 10

A new understanding

I now had an understanding of the Bible that I had never had before, and I began my own Bible study with the help of a concordance. I was amazed to discover how the Bible seemed to explain itself in such a wonderful way. I felt I had discovered a Book with the answers to every question under the sun. It is so full of the wisdom and knowledge of God. I found answers to all the questions I had been asking God for such a long time. Of course, there is still much in the Bible that I do not understand. There is so much hidden treasure, and we can always find something new.

During this time the Lord spoke to me through His word telling me that I should love Him. I began to search the Bible for verses explaining how I could love God as He commanded me. The first verse that spoke to me was John 14: 15: "*If you love Me, keep My commandments."* That frightened me. How could I keep such commandments? Jesus' words in Matthew 22: 37,39,40 made everything clear. *"... You shall love the Lord your God with all your heart, with all your soul, and with all your mind. ... And the second is like it: You shall love your neighbour as yourself. On these two commandments hang all the Law and the Prophets."*

I need only to focus my mind on these two commandments, and in obeying them I would be fulfilling all of God's law. For if I loved God above all, I would live to please Him in obedience to His commands, and if I truly loved those around me I would not wish to harm any of them. Yet I knew that the ability to love them could only come from Him!

This gave me consolation as I felt that God, through His Holy Spirit, had already given me such a love for Himself and for everyone. Of course, we all have ups and downs and, although we enjoy mountain top experiences, we have to go through times of trial when our faith is tested. We have to learn to walk with God and sometimes overcome our fears and unloving attitude to other people. It is a lifelong experience for us to learn to love those who hate us.

Once I was deeply hurt as someone was saying things about me that were not true. One night I cried out desperately to God and when I finally went to sleep I dreamed that my grandmother spoke to me: "Get up and read Matthew Chapter 5 verse 10."

I immediately got up and read the verse, "*Blessed are those who are persecuted for righteousness' sake, for theirs is the Kingdom of heaven.*" I was greatly comforted.

On another occasion I fell prey to criticism and once again was very deeply hurt. When I cried out to God in my distress He impressed upon me once more the truth in Matthew Chapter 5, this time in verses 11 and 12: "*Blessed are you when they revile and persecute you, and say all kinds of evil against you falsely for My sake. Rejoice, and be exceedingly glad; for great is your reward in heaven ...*"

At that time I was unable to rejoice. I was still very troubled, and after praying for God's help, He granted me a vision. The Lord Jesus and I were walking along the pavement beside the church. The path was full of leaves. We were both very hungry and suddenly I saw an apple nestling amidst the leaves. As I stooped down and picked up the apple, I saw that it was rotten except for one little bite-sized piece. I offered up the good part to the Lord, but He said, "No, you take the good part and give me the bad. I can make it whole again, but you cannot."

Whenever I have to undergo criticism or persecution I recall this vision. The Lord is so wise and illustrated many things to His disciples in the Bible which are for our learning. When we forgive and pray for those who hurt us, two things happen. If God knows we are honest, He will release us from the heaviness of our heart and give peace. The one who has hurt us is released from the oppression of our unforgiving spirit. Jesus takes them, like the bad part of the apple, and works in their conscience, convicting them of their wrongdoing until they, in turn, ask for God's forgiveness. He who created perfection can make them whole. So we must learn to forgive and bear no grudges.

I was inspired to study the Bible more closely and understand more deeply. I compiled study notes which helped me to enjoy closer communion with God. His word became as necessary to me as food. My youngest grandson, James, read my notes and wrote a report. It makes me smile every time I read it. He was only eight years old when he penned these words. (Both my grandsons call me "Amsy".)

Amsy's Report

I think that Kamala's report on Jesus' death on the cross had a lot of thought put into it. Every word of it was true. I agree about how much pain he must have been through. I think she is someone who knows a lot about the Bible and she is a very wise person who understands Christianity.

General mark - A* Merit Mark

General comments - Very good – shows understanding

Signed: J. Thanesan.

As I studied the Old Testament, in particular the book of Leviticus, I was astonished to find so many similarities in religious observance between the Jewish and Hindu traditions. The Hindu customs regarding women in childbirth which I have already explained in my experience are very similar to those carried out in the Jewish religion.

My daughter Kanchana with grandsons
James and Simon and myself.

I remember sacrifices being offered in the Hindu temple, usually a goat or chicken. A cow was never offered as it is regarded as sacred. Sacrifices were offered on festive occasions and male goats were specially bred for this purpose. Afterwards the meat was brought home and a big feast was held. These customs eventually faded out, although some ortho-dox Hindus still keep these traditions.

The words of Leviticus 9: 15 outline the Jewish sacrificial ceremony. "*Then he brought the people's offering, and took the goat, which was the sin offering for the people, and killed it, and offered it for sin, like the first.*"

Here we have two religions so similar in practice, but the Bible points to a better way: "*Not with the blood of goats and calves, but with His own blood He entered the Most Holy Place once for all, having obtained eternal redemption.*" (Hebrews 9: 12.) "*For there is one God and one Mediator between God and men, the Man Christ Jesus.*" (1 Timothy 2: 5.) "*Jesus said to him, 'I am the way, the truth and the life. No one comes to the Father except through Me'.*" (John 14: 6.)

Hinduism had no practical relevance to my life. It was not until I found Jesus and experienced His forgiveness for my sins that I found real life and hope.

Hindus believe in philosophy. Every mature Hindu will impart philosophical wisdom to others and, as far as I know, they keep very high moral standards. Astrology, palm reading and looking into the future, predicting signs of evil or good is a great source of consolation to the Hindu. When suffering comes they believe it is largely due to their star sign and planet position, never chance or consequence.

This gives them a false sense of security, accepting unquestioningly what is inevitably due to happen to them. They also have a sense of bearing the consequences of sins from their previous lives, and so are able to patiently endure their burdens.

Conversely, I have found that Christianity offers unique freedom from our burdens. In Matthew 11: 28 Jesus says: "*Come to Me, all you who labour and are heavy laden, and I will give you rest.*" This freedom is only available to those who desire it and who seek after it.

Because I have experienced such freedom I have been given a completely new outlook on life and have found purpose and fulfilment in Jesus. I turned from the darkness of religious ritual and found the light of truth in Jesus. After such deep experiences of Himself and a new and greater understanding of His Word, I longed to share my experiences with others, especially my family in Sri Lanka.

In 1987, my brothers organised a big party back home to celebrate our parents' Diamond Wedding Anniversary. My father was 86 and my mother was 80. I longed to share in the celebrations and tell them of my new-found faith. Unfortunately, I was unable to get annual leave as the hospital was so busy. Although I went to see the manager he would not grant me leave.

I was so frustrated and cried out to God, "Why, O Lord?" But I felt that for some reason the Lord had shut the door. As I continued to pray, the Lord impressed upon my heart that I should wait until the following April.

God's perfect planning gradually became apparent. During this time, when I was working nights in the Intensive Care Unit at Orsett Hospital, my niece, Nalayini, who was living in Surrey, had to undergo a hysterectomy operation. Although the operation was successful, her husband telephoned at 4 a.m. on the morning after to tell me that she had taken a turn for the worse.

"Please, Auntie," he pleaded, "could you come?"

I gained permission to leave immediately for St George's Hospital in Tooting, taking a Bible with me. I had never driven in London before and prayed earnestly as I tentatively weaved in and out of the traffic. With the Lord's help, I arrived at the hospital to find my niece's husband, Raj and brother Satha, waiting anxiously.

They told me that Nalayini had been bleeding profusely and this had led to a cardiac arrest. The doctors and nurses were trying to resuscitate her. She still continued to bleed and after she had revived a little, they took her back to the theatre to repair the damage. Raj and Satha begged me to pray. Although they were not Christians, they believed in prayer. I had never been put on the spot like that before. I sat and prayed silently, "Lord, what do I do now? Please help me, I don't know what to say."

All at once the peace of God filled me and I boldly blurted out, "She is not going to die. She is going to be all right."

Afterwards, Raj told me that he immediately felt a deep peace as if a big burden had been lifted from him.

We watched as the doctors wheeled Nalayini out of the theatre and into ITU where they placed her on a respirator. After a few minutes, the doctor came to speak to Raj.

Tears ran down his face as he took Raj's hand and said, "I am so sorry. She has only a 50-50 chance."

Raj and Satha began to cry and, although I felt so sorry for them, I possessed an inner, unshakable confidence that she would pull through.

It was 8 o'clock in the morning, and I told them to go home and rest while I stayed to pray. I continued in prayer until noon and then went into ITU to see how Nalayini was responding. Just as I entered, to my utmost joy, she started to come round.

"She is over the worst," the nurse said, smiling broadly.

I bent over Nalayini and whispered, "Auntie is here. Don't worry about anything."

Nalayini nodded her head. I was so moved by such evidence of God's goodness. Never before had I seen prayer answered so quickly and effectively. What a wonderful God! Nalayini eventually left the hospital and completely recovered. Now, she is absolutely fit, walks three miles a day and plays badminton.

CHAPTER 11

Sharing the Good News

In April 1988, God granted my desire to visit my family. I was able to obtain leave from work and booked a flight home to Sri Lanka. I was packing my bag and felt I should take a black sari with me. I thought perhaps, as my parents were old, one of them might pass away. I was to learn the real reason later.

During the plane journey, I was reading the Bible and praying when the Lord spoke to me: "When you reach home, say: 'Salvation has come to this house'."

I could not wait to obey His command and longed to share my faith with my family. My brother Mahendran met me at the airport. At that time my parents were living with him.

After moving from their home which had been given to me as a dowry, my parents had been unsettled, living in rented accommodation. In 1979, after my daughter had married, we had all gone to Sri Lanka to visit our family. There was a small plot of land in Jaffna that my sister had urged me to buy long before I left England. My relatives introduced me to a building contractor and I designed a bungalow which was built and paid for within a year. My parents were overjoyed to have a house of their own once again.

Unfortunately, in 1982 there was trouble between the Tamils and the ruling Government. In 1984 Jaffna was bombed and people became homeless, and as a result my family was split up. After spending four happy years in their new home, they had to flee to Colombo, leaving all their furniture and belongings behind. It was a tortuous and difficult journey as there was no public road or rail transport.

We often speak of their house, but as a result of the civil war, no one seemed to know what happened to it. Some say bombs destroyed it and others that all the houses in Tellipalai were bulldozed to the ground. One of my relatives asked, "Why did you spend so much money to build that house for your parents?"

"They enjoyed four happy years in that house, so every penny I spent was worth it. I have no regrets," was my vehement reply.

My brothers feared for our parents' lives and Kandasamy brought them to live in safety in Colombo with Mahendran. So it was to this home, three years later, that Mahendran took me that day, and I did as the Lord had told me.

"Salvation has come to this house," I proclaimed as I entered, but no one took any notice. My parents and my brother Mahendran and his family were completely oblivious to what I was saying, but I was not deterred. A few hours later, two sisters came from the Pentecostal church in Colombo. God had been preparing my family by sending these two sisters prior to my arrival. They had been visiting the family to pray with them and tell them about Jesus. Although my parents respected their religious beliefs and welcomed the sisters into their home, they had no intention of changing their Hindu religion. However, God had prepared the ground for me.

I told the sisters of my experience of salvation. Consequently, they wanted me to give my testimony at their church the following Sunday. I invited my mother to go with me and she accepted.

After listening to my testimony, the pastor invited me to speak at another church on the following Sunday, which was Easter Sunday. There my eldest brother, Kandasamy, came to listen. As a result, he wanted to buy a copy of the Bible. We were only able to obtain a copy of John's Gospel which he took home to read.

I felt such a power and longing within me to share my faith and joy with my family. I told them that the pictures of idols which they worshipped in their prayer room were not real gods. I took all the pictures down and told them the truth about God, that He did not live in the pictures and idols and quoted the relevant scriptures, from Exodus chapter 20: "*You shall have no other gods before Me. You shall not make for yourself a carved image.*"

I explained how Jesus came to die for our sins and show us the way back to God. I told them how God had changed my life and that I was a new person, and began to hold regular Bible studies in the house. They did not know what hurricane force had hit them!

My father was very worried. Once I overheard him talking in the bedroom with my mother. "What do you think about this? How can she take all our pictures down? I would never become a Christian. What do you think?"

"I don't know. We will wait and see," my mother replied.

At that time, many more Tamils had fled from Jaffna to Colombo. They too had lost all their belongings and property and felt very insecure. Mahendran welcomed a few of them into his home, and I held a Bible study with them as well as the family — seventeen in all, each evening. They all listened and asked questions, and so the Lord began to work amongst them.

Kandasamy, my eldest brother, had a very unhappy life and had resorted to drinking to drown his sorrows. In 1985 he became very ill and Mahendran, who is so kind and easy going and always willing to give shelter to anyone in need, agreed to look after him. Mahendran made Kandasamy promise not to drink again. Kandasamy kept his promise for a while. Later, he began to drink again and as a result the family ostracised him.

He was the brother who came to hear my testimony at the Easter Sunday service. He did not stay with me for very long and it was hurting me inside to see him look so haggard when before he had been so handsome. I had always been especially close to Kandasamy and I felt so sorry for him. His wife was living in France with their children, and he had been lodging with a Roman Catholic family.

Before I left Britain, I had written to Kandasamy warning him of the evils of alcohol and how his slavery to the bottle had changed his personality. I told him that I longed to have him as he was before he had fallen prey to such an evil habit. He replied to my letter at great length, parts of which I would like to share with you.

"It gives me immense pleasure to note that you have analysed my life-long problem with expertise, so vividly and so precisely in your four-page letter ... As you have so well penetrated and touched my innermost conscience, I would like to illustrate my position through a small joke. At the entrance to a famous and well patronised bar in a busy town, there hung a small board which often went unnoticed and on which there was a warning which read, 'Alcohol Kills Slowly'. One day this warning caught the eye of a drunk who scribbled underneath, 'So, who is in a hurry anyway?'

"Earlier, right, justice and trust remained the guiding principles of my conduct, and in the forefront of everything was my love and reverence for my family, and my children especially. ... I strongly felt that as I came from obscurity, I would surely go into oblivion ... Therefore, I decided (like that drunk who wrote 'Who is in a hurry anyway') to destroy myself slowly and took refuge in the bottle."

As I read, my heart ached for my favourite brother. The neat hand and clear English prose evoked childhood memories of when Kandasamy would teach English to me and my brothers. He would preside at the table with a ruler at hand to discipline us if we spoke or slacked in any way.

Later, when I was working in the hospital at Innuvil and Kandasamy was working in Colombo, he would teach me English by post. He also visited and brought books to read to me into the early hours. I loved him so much; he was so tireless, so kind and patient.

In April, Hindus celebrate the Tamil New Year, and whilst I was in Sri Lanka the family were preparing for the celebration. They cooked special food which they shared with their neighbours and relatives. On this particular day, they were giving out food to the neighbours and asked me to have some.

"Haven't you forgotten someone?" I asked.

"No," they replied.

"But you are celebrating with your neighbours and have forgotten our own brother, Kandasamy!" I protested.

They looked extremely embarrassed and mumbled, "Oh, well we have run out of food now."

"Then make some more," I insisted.

At this, my sister-in-law set about making some more food. To my utmost joy, we all piled into the van and went to visit Kandasamy. When he saw us coming through the door, he came running to meet us and hugged and kissed each one of us. We gave him the food and his face shone. I thanked the Lord for the spirit of unity. Kandasamy told me he had finished reading John's Gospel and showed an interest in becoming a Christian. It was the Lord who had brought this about; He is the one who unites. We spent some time with Kandasamy before returning home.

I continued holding Bible studies with the family, and Kandasamy's daughter, Dhaya, came to listen. She lived in France and was visiting her father in Sri Lanka, having left her children in the care of her mother. To my great joy, she expressed a desire to become a Christian and be baptised. She told me that she had started to read the Bible and pray. One day whilst she was praying, she had a vision in which she hailed a taxi. As she was in such a hurry, she did not even tell the driver where she wanted to go, but he took her to the exact place. She got out and went to pay the fare, but the driver said, "No, it has been paid."

"Who paid you?" she asked.

"The Lord Jesus," was his reply, and the vision ended.

From then on, she desired to become a Christian and wanted to be baptised while I was in Sri Lanka. We arranged for her to receive preparatory lessons before her baptism, which took place two weeks before I returned home to England. I was so thrilled to see the whole family attending.

Later, Dhaya told me what happened when she went back to her family in France. Her husband, Karuna, picked her up from the airport. As they entered their house she left her suitcase at the doorway and collected every picture of the Hindu gods and goddesses in the house and threw them into the bin.

"Have you gone out of your mind?" Karuna gasped as he looked on incredulously.

Dhaya explained that she had become a Christian and wanted to attend a church every Sunday. She found a church where Sri Lankans worshipped in the Tamil language and Karuna had the unpleasant task of taking her to and from the church by car each Sunday!

One Sunday, Karuna decided to stay outside and wait until the service was over. He became so restless and anxious to know what was going on in the church that he decided to have a peep. The 'peep' became a faltering walk down the aisle and sitting quietly down as the minister said, "Is there anyone here who is not a Christian?" Karuna found himself putting his hand up with many others. The minister invited them to the front for prayer. He prayed that the Holy Spirit might reveal to them the truth about the Lord Jesus.

That night Karuna could not sleep. He felt restless and uncomfortable. He sat on the edge of the bed and lit a cigarette. Suddenly, he saw a vision. The wall in front of him changed into an ocean of water. A hand appeared beckoning him "Come, come to me."

Karuna was so frightened that he rushed out of the room saying, "No, I can't come. I'm not coming!" He finished his cigarette, went back to the bedroom hardly daring to look at the wall, but there was nothing there. He woke Dhaya and told her what had happened.

"Why didn't you say, 'Yes Lord, I will come'?" she chided.

From then on Karuna's life was turned upside down. He started going to church and stopped smoking and drinking. Dhaya telephoned to tell me that Karuna was being baptised the following Christmas Eve. I immediately booked the first available flight to witness such a wonderful event.

Since then Dhaya's three children have all become believers and her mother has become a Christian. Karuna has become an evangelist to his family and friends. His mother, sister and family, his brother and his wife and children have all accepted the Lord Jesus as their Saviour and have been baptised in Sri Lanka.

CHAPTER 12

By the skin of his teeth

Three days after Dhaya's baptism, we had a call from her father, Kandasamy, telling us that he had been admitted into hospital. I immediately went to visit him with Mahendran. Kandasamy's condition was serious; they had diagnosed cirrhosis of the liver. He wanted to tell his son, Thayanandan, who lived in England, so I telephoned to let him know.

Kandasamy's condition deteriorated so quickly that he had to be transferred to the intensive care unit. During this time, Dhaya and I spent most of our time at his bedside. Although he was only semi-conscious, I was able to speak to him about the love of God and how he could even now ask God to forgive his sins and accept Jesus as his Saviour. Some friends came from the church to pray over him.

The following day when Dhaya and I visited him, he was unconscious, and in his pain he was throwing himself around so much that they had to tie his hands and feet to the bed to keep him stable. I was so saddened by this and sat down and cried and prayed.

Then, as I whispered the message of God again in his ear and quietly sang a chorus, his breathing became less laboured and he seemed to calm down. I asked the nurse to untie him. Then God prompted me to baptise him. I was very hesitant to do this as I felt it did not seem right that I, a mere woman and not a church official, should attempt to do this. The prompting became stronger, so I had to obey. I asked the nurse for a wet flannel, which I put over his forehead and prayed aloud, "I baptise you in the name of the Father, the Son and the Holy Spirit."

At that point, his landlady walked into the room. When she saw what was happening she said, "Sister, you are doing the right thing. Your brother wanted to be baptised after he read the Gospel of John which you gave him."

This confirmation brought me immediate peace. The nurse then asked me to leave the room as she had to attend to my brother. Once outside in the corridor, I phoned the church and spoke to an elder, explaining what had happened. She prayed with me on the telephone, asking God to release Kandasamy and take him into His Kingdom.

As we finished praying, the nurse tapped me on the shoulder and whispered, "He has passed away."

Immediately, the Lord spoke in my heart: "I have

got him by the skin of his teeth." ("*My bone clings to my skin and to my flesh, and I have escaped by the skin of my teeth.*" Job 19: 20.)

My joy was inexpressible. Although I felt much sorrow in parting with my dearest brother, it was cushioned by a deep peace and gladness in my heart that Kandasamy was safe in the Kingdom of God. Now I realised why God had asked me to pack a black sari when I left England!

The experience deepened my assurance of eternal life. Perhaps it is not a subject we think too much about, but God goes before us to prepare a place for those that love Him, so that we might be with Him. ("*In My Father's house are many mansions; if it were not so, I would have told you. I go to prepare a place for you.*" John 14: 2.) Many fear death, but in my understanding, death is becoming unconscious to this world and immediately conscious in the presence of God.

My relatives wanted to go through the Hindu rites before my brother's cremation. They sang Hindu hymns and songs and dressed him up in garlands of flowers. On the eighth day after the cremation, they wanted to hold another ritual which is part of the Hindu custom, where they make an effigy of the dead person and dress it up. They would place before it different foods which the person liked when he was alive, then call the priest to come and chant etc.

I objected strongly to this and refused to let it take place. I stressed that it would have been better if they had given him more attention when he was alive. Although they argued about it, God was with me and they eventually gave in. Instead, we invited all those who cared for him and other relatives to a meal. Kandasamy's son came from England and stayed with us. He was very fond of his father and had wept uncontrollably as he carried out the rites of a son. Afterwards we sent some food parcels to the poor.

I had been with my family for five weeks, but it was during the last two weeks that God accomplished the most. My niece was baptised, my brother, Kandasamy, had been baptised and had become a Christian before he died, and at least seventeen other people heard the Gospel in the house. The church held a meeting in the home before I left, inviting neighbours to come and listen to the Gospel. About 25 people came along. I returned to Britain knowing that it had been the Lord's will for me to go to Sri Lanka in April and not before. I felt my mission was accomplished — and yet God had only just begun.

The following year, I received a letter from my mother telling me that she had been baptised in the Indian Ocean at the age of 83!

"I needed the vastness of the ocean to drown all my sins," my mother wrote.

It was such great and unexpected news. My sister-in-law, Mahendran's wife, also became a Christian and was baptised as well as her daughter, who went on to marry a Christian. These were among the seventeen people who had heard the Gospel in my brother's home, and the rest became believers and attended church. I praise God for His goodness in drawing my loved ones to Himself, including my daughter and grandsons in later years.

He kept His promise that He would bring salvation to my family, and to Him be all the glory! There are still those of my family who do not believe, for whom I am continually praying, especially my younger brother, Pathmanathan. He now lives in Australia and is very open-hearted and compassionate. Once, when he was travelling by train from Colombo to Jaffna, a man in the carriage suddenly collapsed and died. Pathmanathan not only carried his body to the car of his waiting relatives at his destination, but went home with them and arranged the funeral!

At the time of writing, my mother is 95 years old. She is now a widow, my father having died in 1991 at the age of 90. Recently, my daughter and family visited her. They took an audio cassette on which I had recorded my testimony and a personal message which she was able to listen to on her personal stereo.

She plays the tape of my testimony to all who visit her, especially Chandran, who I knew when he was a boy. Every time he passes he calls in to listen to the tape. He questions my mother about her faith and asks about the Bible, and she is able to teach him about Jesus. She shares Bible truths with all who come to visit, which thrills and excites me, but she takes it as a matter of course! She is eagerly waiting for me to finish this story so that she can read it before she dies.

(Standing:) Mahendran, Pathmanathan, Kandasamy
(Seated:) Myself, my Father, my Mother, Theivanayaki.

CHAPTER 13

Exercising faith

In 1989, my friend Lilian asked me to accompany her on a pilgrimage to Israel. I gladly accepted and we joined a group from Lilian's church. It proved to be one of the most wonderful experiences I have ever had, just to be where Jesus was born and walk where He had walked. Although some of the group had been there before, for Lilian and myself it was a first.

The places I had read about in the Bible became so much more real and meaningful to my heart. As I stood on the Temple Mount where Solomon's Temple had once stood and is now replaced by a mosque, the Dome of the Rock, Psalm 122 became real: "*I was glad when they said to me, 'Let us go into the house of the Lord.' Our feet have been standing within your gates, O Jerusalem!*"

From Jerusalem, we walked up to the Mount of Olives and looked over the arid terrain strewn with flat-roofed houses, towards the centre of Jerusalem which teemed with traffic tooting continuously. Calls to prayer echoed from the minarets dotted around the city like wailing sirens.

The Kidron Valley stretched beneath us, beyond which lay the tombs of Zechariah and David's son, Absalom. We descended the Mount of Olives to the Garden of Gethsemane and imagined Jesus praying and weeping beneath the great olive tree before His arrest.

We journeyed north to Galilee and were thrilled to cross the lake by boat as Jesus and His disciples had done centuries before. It was so wonderful to feel the peace and joy of the resurrected Lord. We landed in Capernaum and saw the synagogue in ruins where Jesus once read the Scriptures. Then on to Bethlehem and Nazareth to watch craftsmen at work and smell the timber, imagining Jesus as a child working with His father in the carpenter's shop. We gathered so many memories which would prove so precious to me, as a time was coming when my travels were to be severely curtailed.

Two years later, I started to have very bad headaches. I felt giddy, my whole body was in pain and I was unable to see very well. I went to the doctor, but he was unable to make a diagnosis. I struggled on for about seven months. My sight had become so bad I decided to visit the optician. He became immediately concerned as he examined my eyes.

"You must go to the hospital straight away," he said. "There is something seriously wrong!"

His words cut icily into my heart and I hurried to my car. I sat behind the wheel trying to see through the mist in my eyes which had suddenly worsened. I wondered how I could possibly make the journey to the hospital. I slowly and prayerfully let out the clutch and inched gingerly along, literally in blind faith. My heart was beating, my head throbbed and I cried inwardly to the Lord in my desperation.

After what seemed hours of slow and painful edging along the road to Orsett, I drew up outside my doctor's surgery which was opposite the hospital. I groped my way into the surgery and gave the doctor the optician's report. She immediately arranged for me to be admitted to hospital.

I telephoned my friend Lilian who was a nurse at the hospital, and she took me to the Casualty Department. We had worked together in the Intensive Care Unit at Orsett Hospital where Lilian was a sister. She is such a caring person who is always ready to help anyone in need. She had devoted her life to looking after her mother who was wheelchair bound. I will never forget her kindness that day. She waited with me until I was admitted.

I gave her my keys to collect my belongings from my flat and she phoned my daughter. I was sent to have a CT scan. I experienced more nerve-racking moments of waiting until the results came through. The scan was finally reported as normal and the

Registrar talked to the Consultant, who in turn suggested it could be a pituitary problem. They sent me to a neurological hospital in London to have an MRI scan. I was diagnosed as having a pituitary adenoma, i.e. a tumour on the brain, involving the pituitary gland.

I felt numb with shock as my son-in-law drove me back to Orsett Hospital with the results of the scan, and the doctors told me to go home and wait until they could make arrangements with the hospital in London to have the operation. They advised me not to be on my own, but to stay with my daughter and her family. They told my daughter that if I became unconscious she should phone for an ambulance to take me straight to the London hospital.

Throughout that week I felt totally devastated and alone, although I had the comfort of my family around me. This was something I had to face on my own, yet I was not alone. The Lord was with me and I drew great strength and comfort from this knowledge.

I was admitted to the Royal London Hospital, Whitechapel, the following week in May 1991. Before I became ill, I had received HSA health insurance papers through the post which I glanced at with disinterest and put away in a drawer. A little while later, during December, I decided to join the scheme. When I was admitted to hospital the following year, I could see God's providential hand had been at work, as all my expenses were covered by the insurance down to the smallest detail. I praise God who has always provided for my needs.

Just before the tumour was discovered, I had attended a Bible study where someone spoke on exercising faith. At the time, I felt strongly that God was speaking to me. When the tumour was diagnosed this thought came back to me, but I was at a loss to know exactly how I should exercise faith. Should I go back home in faith that God would heal me directly, or should I accept the medical care and undergo surgery as planned? How should I exercise my faith? I was in a complete quandary.

As I entered the neurological ward of the Royal London Hospital I saw patients who had undergone similar operations to their brain. Some had their heads shaved and some were paralysed. This had a devastating effect on me. I had been working as a general nurse and had no knowledge of neuro-surgery. When I saw these patients I suddenly became aware of the possible effects of the operation.

I felt suddenly alone and lay pondering the worst. A darkness seemed to envelop me and I could see no light on the horizon. The tune of a chorus echoed faintly in the recesses of my mind. It gradually became clearer and I recognised the strains of a familiar chorus:

"Have Thine own way, Lord! Have Thine own way!

Thou art the Potter; I am the clay.
Mould me and make me after Thy will,
While I am waiting, yielded and still."

The words brought peace and I yielded my life into the hands of the Potter.

I searched in my bedside cabinet for a pad and pencil and drew a picture of a clay pot broken and chipped and full of errors. Underneath I wrote, "Man is made up full of errors, cracked and imperfect like this jar. It is ugly and not useful to anyone or to itself. It cannot hold water, but will constantly leak. Can a jar like this be made perfect? If so, who could do it? No one but a potter. He will first have to smash the jar to pieces, crunch it and make a fresh lump of clay out of it. When it is ready, the potter puts it on the wheel and makes a perfect jar."

Then I drew a picture of a perfect jar filled with the Spirit of God. I wrote underneath, "Now there are no errors. It is perfect. It can hold water and others can use it. This is how Jesus lived and showed us how to live. Do we want to be a perfect vessel or an imperfect one? No one is perfect, but when we submit ourselves to God, He will break us. Then like the potter, He will renew us and transform us. He fills us with the Holy Spirit, making us perfect that we might shine all the time."

One of the Christian nurses on the ward saw the drawing and exclaimed, "Why, that's lovely!"

She called two of the other nurses. When they

saw it they all gave me a hug and said, "We must put it on the notice board."

The next day I was transferred to the private wing, as my bed was needed for an emergency patient. My daughter was with me when the consultant came to see me. I explained my fears and asked him about any likely complications from the operation. He told me that my head would have to be shaved and my skull opened to reach the tumour. Also, I had to face the possibility of becoming paralysed, losing my speech or losing my sight.

As he faced me with all these possibilities, I became more and more fearful, and for the first time since learning of the existence of the tumour, I started to weep. I put my arms around my daughter and together we sobbed and cried.

"You haven't cried so far, Mum. It will do you good to cry," Kanchana said between her sobs.

Even as I cried, I heard the words in my heart, "Exercise faith."

After the consultant had left and my daughter had returned home, I lay in bed, continuing to wonder how I could exercise faith. I needed to make a decision. The dilemma made me restless. I prayed earnestly and felt an urgent need to talk to a fellow Christian and seek advice. I was soon to realise that God's hand had been at work in having me placed in a private room. I not only had the luxury of a television, but my own private telephone as well! Later that afternoon, the telephone rang. I was overjoyed to hear Claire, a friend from church, on the other end of the line.

"Claire," I exclaimed, "you have rung at just the right time. I am in such a dilemma. I don't know whether I should go ahead with surgery or return home, trusting God to heal me. I know God wants me to exercise faith, but I am not sure exactly how He wants me to do this."

Claire reminded me of John Bunyan's story, "Pilgrim's Progress" when Christian had to go through a narrow passage to reach the Palace Beautiful. He saw two lions in front of him and was afraid and tempted to go back. But the porter of a lodge en route called to him not to turn back. "Is thy strength so small? Fear not the lions for they are chained and are placed there for trial of faith where it is, and for discovery of those that have none: keep in the midst of the path, and no hurt shall come unto thee." Christian went safely through on his journey to Zion.

As soon as Claire mentioned that story, I knew what I had to do. I would go through the operation trusting that I would meet God at the other end, even if it meant death and Zion. I just knew I had to submit myself totally to His divine will. I thanked Claire for her timely help.

All my fears disappeared and I was filled with great joy and peace. I thanked God for prompting Claire to ring. When friends came to visit me, I watched their sadness turn to surprise and wonderment when they witnessed my peace and serenity. My outward calm was born of an inner peace and acceptance of God's will. I wrote in my diary: "Faith is believing in things unseen. Exercising faith is believing that the unseen God can perform His will within us when we submit ourselves totally and unconditionally into His hands."

As I felt that God might take me home, I made the necessary preparations. I gave away what little jewellery I had and wrote out my testimony, which I gave to my daughter to read at my funeral. Kanchana was devastated at the prospect, but some time later she told me that she had cried to the Lord and He had given her a sense of peace which enabled her to cope.

On the day before the operation, my very close friends, David and Cathy Benton, came to pray with me in the hospital chapel and we shared communion. David and Cathy are always there in time of need, praying for me and giving me practical and spiritual support. I remember when my grandson, Simon, was ill, they and their friends at Purfleet Baptist Church were a wonderful support in prayer.

As we walked back from the chapel, we met the consultant in the doorway of the ward. He looked at me thoughtfully and said, "I am going to operate through the nose rather than your skull, so you will not need to have your head shaved."

"That's an amazing answer to prayer!" said my friends.

I walked back to my bed feeling overjoyed and safe in the knowledge that, having given everything totally into God's hands, He was showing me such kindness. My skull would not have to be opened and I would be able to keep my hair and my dignity come what may! I will never forget the lesson I learned that day. Total submission will always result in immeasurable blessing. In relinquishing all my worldly possessions and totally submitting to His will, I felt the richest person alive!

During my stay in the hospital, Peter, the Church of England chaplain, visited me daily. He often had a little prayer with me. I was so pleased to see so many Christian faces — a Church of England nun who was so radiant and exuberant, and two of the nurses with whom I was able to share Christian fellowship. I was also able to share my faith with some of the other patients. When they asked me why I was so happy, I would tell them that God was looking after me and that He was able to look after them if they trusted in Him.

On the day of the operation, at my request, Peter came to give me communion. It was Ascension Day, 9th May 1991. I felt I might be going to the Lord on such a special day! On my way to the operating theatre I listened to a Graham Kendrick worship tape on my personal stereo. Although I was feeling very drowsy, I managed to sing "Shine Jesus Shine", as the trolley trundled along the corridor.

My daughter and son-in-law walked alongside

looking very distraught and quite untouched by my singing. Thanesh cried and kissed me, saying, "All the best. You will be all right."

Kanchana could not keep back the tears, but I remained in a state of euphoria, partly as a result of the pre-med injection, but mainly because I thought that I might soon be with my precious Saviour!

After six to seven hours of oblivion in surgery, I awoke to a voice which sounded like an angel from heaven. In fact, it was the nursing sister in intensive care, who was so kind and understanding, seeing to my every need. Then I heard my daughter's voice and knew I could not be in heaven but had come through the operation. The nurse kept asking me questions to evaluate my level of consciousness. I vividly remember her first question: "What's the name of the Prime Minister?"

"John Major," was my immediate reply.

The Lord had brought me through and my only visible scar was on my thigh where they had taken a small bone to repair my nose.

CHAPTER 14

His grace is sufficient

When recovering from the operation I was greatly uplifted by the many cards, get well wishes and flowers which I received from my family, my personal friends, from those at church and from the hospital where I worked. I received excellent care and attention from the consultant and doctors and all the staff who looked after me.

There was just one small drawback. Fluid from the brain started to trickle through the back of my nose and down to my throat, making me sick. This was because the wound inside my forehead would not heal properly. The consultant came to see me and said that he wanted to do a lumbar puncture in order to relieve the pressure. This would prevent the fluid trickling down my nose and allow the wound to heal. The mention of "lumbar puncture" brought new fears, as it is such a painful process.

"Could you please give me three days to pray for healing?" I asked the consultant. It was a Friday and the consultant smiled and said, "OK, we'll leave it until Monday."

Kanchana and I prayed earnestly throughout the weekend and I was careful to restrict my head movements to prevent aggravation to the leakage of fluid.

When the consultant came to see me on the Monday morning I exclaimed, "My prayers have been answered, the fluid has stopped trickling down my nose!"

I waited anxiously for his reaction. He looked down at me very thoughtfully then smiled and said, "Ah, you have escaped the lumbar puncture then!"

I was overjoyed and praised and thanked the Lord, giving Him all the glory.

After 21 days of radiotherapy treatment, I was given further X-rays and then discharged with lifelong medication to compensate for the loss of the pituitary gland. With great disappointment, the consultant explained that I would be partially sighted because of the effects of the pressure of the tumour on the nerves that affect the sight.

On the day my daughter came to take me home, I felt very strange. When I entered the hospital I had relinquished all my worldly possessions, having totally submitted my whole life to God. I had expected to go home to the Lord. Now I had to adjust to the idea of going back to my old life. I had to take back all those things that I had relinquished. This gave me a different attitude towards my possessions. They did not mean a lot to me before, but now I had an even lighter hold upon them. I felt unsure of what life held for me in the future, yet I had a deep sense of peace and joy as my daughter helped me into her car. As we drove along, I told Kanchana that her car seemed like a golden chariot sent by God to take me home!

When we reached my daughter's house, I was thrilled to see a large drawing of a heart on the front door, bearing the message, "Welcome Home Grandma", which my grandsons had made. It was all so comfortable, just like my own home. I groped my way to an armchair in the lounge and sat down. I could hear the children's voices but could not see them as my eyes were so blurred.

"Look at our goldfish in the bowl, Amsy", they cried.

I turned but could see nothing. They helped me find my way into the garden, but I couldn't even see the flowers which I knew would be in full bloom. I wanted to cry, but went back inside desperately trying to control my emotions. My daughter had given strict instructions to the boys not to leave any of their toys around on the floor that might trip me up.

They led me upstairs to my bedroom which my daughter had beautifully prepared. It felt cosy and warm and Kanchana showed me where a flask of hot water and coffee stood on the bedside table. She had done everything to make me comfortable. The whole room was filled with the beautiful fragrance of flowers and my daughter had stuck hundreds of get well cards to the wall. I hugged Kanchana and said through my tears, "It feels just like heaven. It is so beautiful."

The time eventually came to return to my flat, although Kanchana did not want me to go home so soon.

"Please, I must go back and learn to be independent again," I insisted.

When the moment came to step inside my flat, I was filled with a feeling of desolation and helplessness. Yet as I closed the door and walked down the hallway to the lounge I could feel the Lord's presence. This was my real home where I had spent so many hours with the Lord. This was where I had met the Lord in such a special way. I felt comforted and knew He was there to help me. I tried to peer through the filmy haze which still covered my eyes and found it difficult to find my way around.

I had every intention of going back to my job, but the hospital decided it would be impossible and gave me early retirement on the grounds of ill health. At first I was devastated as I began to realise how difficult it was to cope with restricted vision. My daughter was very apprehensive about my living on my own, but I resolved to spend time with God and find out what He had in store for me. Having been independent since I was 18 years old I did not wish to become a burden to anyone. I was determined with God's help to make the best of the rest of my life.

I received no help or advice from anyone on how to cope with my disabilities in a practical sense. I was frustrated and desperate to know what to do.

As I spent time in prayer, I remembered other times when God had been so real and answered my prayers. My thoughts dwelt on the time when I had been giving a friend a lift to the airport and the car had broken down.

My friend became frantic as she thought she was going to miss her flight. I remained amazingly calm and bowed my head in prayer. "Please Lord, send someone to help us," I cried in my heart. Within seconds a car drew up alongside and a kindly looking man got out. He lifted the bonnet and knew immediately what the problem was, and swiftly solved the mystery beneath. We thanked him profusely and he was gone, as quickly as he came. I was convinced God had sent His angel to help us. Now as I sat in the quietness of my flat, I knew He would never let me down and that He would help me through.

When I had been staying with my daughter, I had a dream in which an angel was sitting in a courtyard. I came down the steps and the angel spoke, "You must sell your car and settle the debts on your credit card."

I was so taken aback and asked, "How do you know about my credit card or my car?"

The angel replied, "The Lord told me to tell you."

When I woke up the next morning I thought, "What a strange dream." As my habit was, I switched on my personal stereo to listen to my Bible reading tape and was astounded to hear the words, "*Owe no one anything except to love one another, for he who loves another has fulfilled the law.*" (Romans 13: 8.)

I was amazed and took this as confirmation that God had spoken regarding selling my car. I explained everything to my daughter and suggested that I should do as the Lord had told me in the dream. I asked my son-in-law to put an advert in their local newspaper. We had received no reply to the advert before I left.

However, during my first week in my flat, my daughter telephoned to tell me that someone had called about the car. They arranged for the man to look at the car and he immediately asked my son-in-law how much he wanted. He told the man that it was worth £1,650. Without even a test drive, the man took out the correct money, gave it to Thanesh and immediately drove the car away.

When my daughter told me they had sold it for £1,650, I was amazed, as that was the exact amount I owed on my credit card! I was able to settle the debt, cut up the credit card and knew the Lord did not want me to get into debt in this way again.

The Lord continued to meet my daily needs as I

faced life with restricted sight. Someone suggested that I contact the Royal Institute for the Blind. They were most helpful. They sent me a white walking stick and a lady came to train me to walk with the stick. They also provided me with a talking book service, — books recorded onto audio tape, and special money dispensers to help me differentiate between coins when shopping. It took six months to a year for my eyesight to improve. Although my left eye was badly impaired, the sight on the left side of my right eye became sharp and clear and I was able to cope more easily with my daily chores.

The Lord has given me many friends who are so kind and helpful to me in time of need. There are times when I feel I am taking advantage of them, but they are so kind and generous, and I would not know what to do without their help. I thank God for such friends and glorify Him.

I was lost without my car, and I joined Socketts Heath Baptist Church which was nearer to my home. There I have found much love and warmth and look forward to going to church on Sundays. On Wednesday mornings I lead the Ladies' Bible Study Group.

My friend Ruth often took me up to Westminster Chapel to attend the School of Theology. The more I learn from God's Word the more I want to learn. I have been greatly helped in this by purchasing a set of Bible audio tapes and a hand-held electronic Bible, as I am unable to read for more than half an hour with the aid of glasses and a large magnifying glass. And so the Lord has undertaken and my faith is strengthened each day as I grow in the Lord.

Knowing how much I like to learn about God's Word, a friend asked me along to her church to a class in theology. It was a very high Church of England and the minister was taking the lectures. He was teaching about the birth of Christ.

As I listened, I realised he was not teaching the truth as I knew it in the Bible.

"The virgin birth is a fallacy," he proclaimed, and went on to say that the Gospels of Mark and Luke should never be included in the Bible.

"Who is this Luke?" he said mockingly.

I was becoming more and more uncomfortable as I listened to his erroneous teaching.

"The Hindus have got it right. God incarnate. God was born to a woman, but not without Joseph," he continued. "Prophecy refers to a 'young woman' not a 'virgin'."

Although I had attended a service at this church with my friend, this was the first time I had heard their teaching. My spirit quickened within me.

I put up my hand and said, "Please excuse me. I am only a visitor here, but I want to say that I believe the Bible. Jesus' birth was a virgin birth. Mary conceived Jesus by the Holy Spirit and He is the Son of God. I have attended the School of Theology at Westminster Chapel. They taught that there was no word in Hebrew for 'virgin' and so she was called 'young woman'."

The person next to me got up and asked, "What is the Hebrew word for virgin?"

"I'm afraid I don't know," the minister replied.

He did not seem to realise that the Hebrew word 'alma' used in Isaiah Chapter 7 was normally understood to mean 'virgin'.

"Excuse me," I continued. "No one has the right to remove anything from the Bible. Jesus said: 'Heaven and earth shall pass away, but my words shall not pass away'.

"I have attended your service at church and I noticed that when a person finishes reading God's Word to the congregation, he picks up the Bible, kisses it, lifts it up and says: 'This is the Word of God'. Do you do this when you read the Gospels of Mark and Luke?"

There was a corporate, sharp intake of breath and I felt the united condemnation of everyone present. How dare I attack their age-old rituals!

Still I carried on my defence of God's truth. "Please don't talk to me about incarnation. I was a Hindu and it is truth about the deity of Christ that converted me."

"Why don't you join us next week? We will be discussing incarnation," invited the minister.

"No thank you," I replied, and as I walked out people approached me, but I felt I had outstayed my welcome.

"Let's go home," I said to my friend.

As we were driving back I said, "He is walking on dangerous ground. He is teaching heresy."

She had to agree. I was reminded of 2 Peter 2: 1: "*But there were also false prophets among the people, even as there will be false teachers among you, who will secretly bring in destructive heresies ...*"

I thank the Lord that when we become a Christian, through the Holy Spirit we know the Truth and "*the Truth shall make you free*" (John 8: 32) liberating us from all error.

CHAPTER 15

The Ideal Husband

I awoke one morning with a wonderful sense of the Lord's peace and nearness and the words, "The Lord is my husband," on my lips. I mused on how He had always been there for me, loving, guiding, directing and protecting me all through the years, even at times when I was not even aware of His intervention.

I thought of the time in 1989 when I had received a notification from the local council suggesting I might like to buy my council flat. I prayed, "Lord, if you want me to buy it, I will."

A little while later, I was introduced to a Hindu financial adviser who offered to help me buy the flat. I thought it was the Lord's doing and He was giving me the go-ahead to buy it.

The man rang a few days later and said, "I am very sorry, but no one will give you a mortgage."

He called at my flat to return the mortgage application form. "I cannot understand it," he said, "I have always been successful with everyone else. You are the first failure!"

He seemed so disappointed. "Never mind," I said. "It doesn't matter. It is just not meant to be."

He looked at me, full of concern and asked, "How do you manage on your own?"

"I have faith in the Lord. Without Him I could not cope," I replied.

"I am glad you have faith," he said. "I have got faith. I worship Sai-Ba-Ba."

My heart sank and I suddenly became very wary. Since he had been following Sai-Ba-Ba he told me he had become very prosperous. He offered every mortgage application to a picture of Sai-Ba-Ba and prayed to him and every one was successful!

I shivered as I had an awful vision of him waving my mortgage application before Sai-Ba-Ba, remembering God's Word in Leviticus 26:1, *"You shall not make idols for yourselves; neither a carved image nor a sacred pillar shall you rear up for yourselves ... for I am the Lord your God."*

"And yours failed!" he exclaimed, completely mortified.

I rejoiced in my heart! Thank God, it had failed! The Lord had protected me. After he left, I was overwhelmed by the love of God. He had defended my interests when I was not even aware of the danger.

The next morning, the Lord urged me to go along to Barclays Bank and apply for a mortgage. I telephoned and made an appointment for that afternoon. I felt a peace as I made my request. Without any hesitation they granted me a mortgage, yet the Hindu adviser had told me he had been turned down by them. I seemed to float out of the bank saturated with the peace of God and praising Him in my heart.

Again, just over two years ago, God met my financial needs in a marvellous way. I still lived in the same high rise flat on the second floor, and felt I would like to live on the ground floor owing to my increasing physical disabilities. I was not sure that I would be able to sell it for the full market price and did not have the courage to make a definite move.

Just before Christmas 1999, I summoned the courage to call an estate agent. It was a step of faith and my daughter was as surprised as I was that I should make such a leap in the dark.

When I returned from spending Christmas at my daughter's, the estate agent rang to tell me that a lady wanted to view the flat. I never thought much about it, but when the lady came she immediately fell in love with it and wanted to buy it. She was the only one who came to view and within a short time she had bought the flat and moved in. It had all happened so quickly that I had not been able to find alternative accommodation. My friend Ruth kindly let me stay with her while I looked for a suitable property.

Now I lay in my new ground floor flat, musing on God's goodness. Again, I had been able to afford a small mortgage and was able to purchase a comfortable flat in pleasant surroundings with good and helpful neighbours.

The Lord has always been faithful in providing for my material needs. I remembered the time when I first read about tithing my income. I wondered how I could possibly afford to part with ten percent of my income each month. At that time when I was working as an SEN I received £800 per month. "How can I possibly part with £80 and meet all my expenses?" I wondered.

I spent much time in prayer before I finally decided to tithe my income. I wrote out a cheque for £80 in readiness to place in the church offering. As I drove to church the following Sunday, a battle raged within me.

"If you give all that money, how will you be able to cope for the rest of the month?" one half of me was saying. The other half replied, "If you do not tithe you will not be obedient to the Word of God."

I could not concentrate on the service. My mind was completely taken over by the thought of giving the cheque. I could not wait for the time when the offering plate came round. When the moment finally came, I closed my eyes and put the cheque onto the plate. Immediately I was enveloped in a wonderful peace and felt as if I was being lifted up high.

I did not realise until later that God was rewarding my obedience with such great blessing. During the following month, the money left in my bank account proved more than adequate for my needs with some to spare. God always blesses me when I give, although I do not give with that motive, but wholeheartedly in love to Him, and He has always met my needs.

"The Lord is my husband," I whispered that morning as I continued to muse on His goodness in providing me with my new home. I turned to read my booklet, "Daily Light". "I am Thy Husband" the heading for that day's reading shone out. It was unbelievable! It went on, *For your Maker is your husband* ..." (Isaiah 54: 5). As a member of the church, the Bride of Christ, I could claim Him as my husband.

I remembered the time when I experienced the baptism of the Holy Spirit. I had bathed in pure, crystal clear water and felt like a bride adorned in a white garment. Then the incredible confirmation as I played the tape Peter had given to me at the time and heard the words of the song, "Take His hand you lovely bride!"

The tears began to flow. " *'For the Lord has called you like a woman forsaken and grieved in spirit, like a youthful wife when you were refused,' says your God.*" (Isaiah 54:6.) Hadn't the Lord been my husband all the way along, even when I did not know Him as I lay with Kumar's hands around my throat? He had protected me from Kumar's pursuing footsteps. When marital bliss had eluded me, He was there to comfort and restore. When I had wandered far from Him, He had drawn me back to Himself with the cords of love. When I faced death on the operating table, again, the Lord had been there for me, protecting, loving and upholding me.

My condition has deteriorated and I have to cope with impaired vision and the side-effects of medication, developing osteoporosis as well as a slipped disc. I have been under the care of an excellent professor at St Bartholomew's Hospital since 1991. He is one of the best.

I have been able to look after myself because of the treatment I received. The Lord is good, providing me with such care. He has never let me down. I will always trust in Him, for I know that He who has led me thus far will never leave me nor forsake me. People ask me if I feel lonely. "No, never," is always my immediate reply. "Because He is always there with me, loving, caring, providing, protecting: my Lord, my husband."